THE

# *Coffeehouse*

# INVESTOR

# THE
# *Coffeehouse*
## INVESTOR

HOW TO BUILD WEALTH

IGNORE WALL STREET

AND GET ON WITH YOUR LIFE

# BILL SCHULTHEIS

LONGSTREET
Atlanta, Georgia

Published by LONGSTREET PRESS, INC.,
a subsidiary of Cox Newspapers,
a subsidiary of Cox Enterprises, Inc.
2140 Newmarket Parkway
Suite 122
Marietta, Georgia 30067

This publication is designed to provide accurate and authoritative information in regard to the subject matter covered. It is sold with the understanding that neither the author nor the publisher is engaged in rendering legal, accounting, or other professional service. If legal advice or other expert assistance is required, the services of a competent professional person should be sought.

S&P 500 Index is a registered trademark of the Standard and Poor's Corporation. Wilshire 5000 Index is a registered trademark of Wilshire & Associates. Russell 2000 Index is a registered trademark of the Frank Russell Company. Used with permission.

Printed in the United States of America

1st printing, 1999

Library of Congress Catalog Card Number: 98-066361

ISBN: 1-56352-600-X

Book and cover design by Burtch Bennett Hunter

# ACKNOWLEDGMENTS

If this book provides any assistance to investors, it is because of the comments, criticisms and encouragement received from readers of early drafts. Those who work and teach in the investment arena, most notably Gary Hirata, Sabrina Seward, Frank Bosone, Emily Palmgren, and Dennis Vogt, were especially helpful in their critical reviews of the book (though they might not have agreed with its entire content). Also, special thanks to Maureen and Tim Travaille, Sue Bridenstine, John Hersman, Andrea Driessen, Bill Hoover, Norva Osborn, John Schneider, Kremiere Boone, Bob Anderson, Petr Sovcov, Cheryl Wagner, everyone at Betty Jane Narver's house, and, most importantly, my mother and father, Anne and Harold Schultheis, for their unending interest and support.

This book would still be a rough manuscript if it weren't for the remarkable foresight of my agent, Richard Valcourt, and especially Suzanne De Galan, the world's greatest editor. As senior editor at Longstreet Press, her liberal use of the red pen only matched her passion for this project. Thank you both.

To May
with gratitude

# CONTENTS

# THE

# *Coffeehouse*

# I N V E S T O R

AFTER THIRTEEN YEARS OF WORKING WITH RETAIL and institutional accounts for a major Wall Street firm in Seattle, Washington, I decided to take a break. That's how this book came about. In discussions with people from all over the Pacific Northwest, I discovered that for every person who is caught up in the daily activities of Wall Street, there are many more who don't want to spend one ounce of energy on it but still demand a successful investment portfolio. These are the people who are passionately involved with their families and careers and enjoy spending their creative energies in places other than the stock market. For these investors, an investment story much different from Wall Street's traditional story needs to be told.

As global markets become more uncertain and sources of financial information proliferate, there is a common belief that increased time and attention to one's investments is required to successfully navigate among 15,000 stocks and mutual funds when building and maintaining an investment portfolio. Nothing could be further from the truth. In fact, it has been shown time and again that excessive attention to investment portfolios combined with advice from stock market experts frequently results in sub-par portfolio performance. Yet many of the people I talked with were astonished to hear this; that is, until I shared with them the story of *The Coffeehouse Investor*.

The fact is, there *are* ways to simplify your investment decisions when building a sophisticated portfolio. With just a minimum of effort you can learn to implement these steps and begin the gratifying process of building wealth, ignoring Wall Street and getting on with your life. As you do so, you will discover that the real benefit to simplifying your investment decisions is that you are able to focus more attention on areas of your life that enrich you the most.

It is early Friday morning and I'm sitting at the corner table of my favorite coffeehouse, finishing this preface. As I search inward for inspiration, I stare out the window and see that the front-page headline of the daily newspaper, propped on the sidewalk stand, is screaming, "RUSSIAN ECONOMY SOCKS DOW – market sees 357-point plunge." Finally, something to divert our attention from the financial crisis in Japan. Or is it Malaysia? Or North Korea? I forget. Meanwhile, the weatherman is predicting nothing but sunshine for the weekend. With a forecast like that, who has time to fret about who's socking whom? This is Seattle. I'm outta here.

Bill Schultheis
August 1998

# *1* THE COFFEEHOUSE INVESTOR

YOU ARE ABOUT TO EMBARK ON A JOURNEY THAT will change the way you invest forever. Along the way we will talk about things like pitching tents and pumpkin pies, because even though building and maintaining a successful investment portfolio today is essential for you to achieve your financial goals tomorrow, we will discover that the simple things in life, like pitching tents and pumpkin pies, are much more important to your investment success than the hype and hysteria of Wall Street, which never makes much sense anyway.

This journey is for everyone — long-time stock market investors as well as beginners — people who can't afford to make a mistake because their financial goals of tomorrow depend on making the right decisions today.

In our efforts to do the right thing with our investment decisions today, though, it's easy to get caught up in the empty words of Wall Street and do lots of wrong things. Well, if there is one place in your life where you don't want to make a mistake it is with your investment decisions, because when it comes to realizing a financial goal someday, if you make a mistake here you won't get a second chance.

I must caution you though: This investment journey will not show you how to pick hot funds and cool stocks, analyze balance sheets, predict business cycles or forecast interest rates. This investment journey simply reveals the three principles of investing and explains why these principles are infinitely more important to your investment success than all the "stock market experts" who try to convince us they know more than we do about all this hot and cool stuff.

In fact, we will discover that one of the requirements for a successful journey is to ignore the "stock market experts" of today in much the same way Aristotle ignored the "flat world experts" 2,400 years ago when suggesting that the earth was round.

Oh by the way, the last time I climbed Mt. Rainier, I stopped just short of the 14,410-foot summit to drink some water and eat some food, and while hanging onto the side of a glacier at about five in the morning I looked over my shoulder (briefly, because I suffer from acrophobia) and saw the sun . . .

rise . . .

and somewhere between Canada to the north and Oregon to the south, I think I detected a slight curve on the earth's horizon.

Now, I am not one to imply there is any correlation whatsoever between the flat earth experts of yesterday and the stock market experts of today, but I will say, unequivocally, that stock market acrophobia, which is fueled in large part by stock market experts, causes many investors to make investment mistakes they are sure to regret when it comes time to retire.

Whether the earth is flat or round doesn't matter much anymore. What does matter is that most of us get up in the morning, put on our working shoes and go to work,

meeting deadlines,
raising children,
learning new technologies,
building careers,
attending school functions,
keeping up with the competition

and generally giving it all we've got.

For most of us, somewhere between the chaos of giving it all we've got today and achieving a financial goal tomorrow lies the daunting task of building and maintaining a successful investment portfolio.

It's hard enough putting a successful investment plan in place amidst the chaos of giving it all we've got every day. But when our efforts to do so come face-to-face with a financial industry that pretends to have all the right answers, there is a tendency to feel like we are slowly sliding off the side of a glacier. . . .

As the world continues to gently spin 'round and 'round, as the days turn into nights and back into days again, our financial goals that seem so far away get closer and closer. The problem is, the world spins so gently, and we are so busy, that it's easy to put off dealing with far-away financial goals, especially when we have the misconception that dealing with something so far away means sorting through thousands of mutual funds, hundreds of advisors and dozens of financial magazines . . .

when all we really have the energy for is dealing with today.

That's why, with our lives so busy and our financial goals so far away, it's critical that, in addition to meeting deadlines, raising children and keeping up with the competition, we learn about the three fundamental principles of investing. Once we do this we can ignore Wall Street and get on with our lives, secure in the knowledge that by implementing the three fundamental principles of investing, our portfolios will be ready for us when we are ready for them.

Focusing on what really counts and ignoring everything else is a major step in any successful journey, because it is easy to get caught up in irrelevant things and follow along with the crowd. Then, even though you begin to notice that what you are doing is not getting you any closer to your goal, it is difficult to change your actions, especially when you see everyone else continuing to do the same thing.

For instance, one of my goals was to break eighty in golf. I practiced and practiced and practiced some more. I could not break eighty. Then one day I played golf with a woman twice my age and half my weight, who not only broke eighty, but shared with me the secret for doing so. After playing eighteen holes of golf on an old public course in West Seattle, she looked at me and said, "The problem with you is, you can't make your four-foot putts."

There's nothing like someone stating the obvious.

From then on, instead of going to the driving range to practice my driver, I went to the putting green to practice my four-foot putts.

Before long, I broke eighty.

Had I never run into that delightful woman who cleared up my misconception that the secret to breaking eighty was hitting a perfect driver, I would still be practicing my driver and ignoring the most important thing of all — my four-foot putts.

It's not easy to go against the grain of popular opinion, especially when you show up at the putting green with your putter while everyone else is at the driving range, smacking their drivers. The same is true when building a successful portfolio — the challenge is to go against the grain of Wall Street by ignoring much of what they throw our way and focusing exclusively on the investment equivalent of four-foot putts —

or what I call the three fundamental principles of investing:

## asset allocation
## approximating the stock market average
## saving

*Asset allocation* means choosing the best combination of stocks, bonds and cash to provide you with the greatest chance of achieving your financial goal with the least amount of risk.

*Approximating the stock market average* means making sure your stock market investments are doing at least as well as what the stock market as a whole is doing. (That is, if the stock market is up 2 percent, your stock market investments should be up 2 percent. If the stock market is up 33 percent, your stock market investments should be up 33 percent.)

*Saving* means knowing how much money you need to set aside each month to reach your financial goal and eventually saving it.

The important thing about *asset allocation, approximating the stock market average* and *saving* is that these three principles are in our control. That is important, because we will see that when we focus on Wall Street, things that are out of our control, such as weekly economic numbers, quarterly earnings reports and year-end mutual fund summaries, tempt us to fiddle around with our investments instead of leaving well enough alone.

Speaking of leaving well enough alone, I find it interesting that less than 10 percent of the millionaires in this country consider themselves "active" traders, and 42 percent of the millionaires of this country make less than one transaction per year in their investment portfolios.[1]

Not one transaction per hour,
not one transaction per day,
not one transaction per week,
not one transaction per month . . .

1. Thomas J. Stanley and William D. Danko, *The Millionaire Next Door* (Atlanta, Ga.: Longstreet Press, 1996).

less than one transaction per year.

Maybe, just maybe, the millionaires of this country have discovered that the more they leave well enough alone and get on with their lives, pursuing their dreams and fulfilling their passions, the better off they and their portfolios will be.

On the other hand, Wall Street types have a tendency to portray this world of investing as fun, exciting and full of busy portfolios. To them, what could be better than waking up each morning, logging onto the Internet after reading *The Wall Street Journal*, then calling Stan the stockbroker and instructing him to buy a little of this and sell a little of that, and please do it immediately because you don't want to miss out on this great investment opportunity that is here today and gone tomorrow, and oh boy,

isn't this fun,
isn't this exciting,
isn't this luxurious . . .

and isn't life grand.

But for those of us who are greeted each morning with children to be fed and dressed for school, and who are completing projects for a ten o'clock seminar; running to catch a bus, train or automobile; and hoping for an extra three minutes to stop by the local coffeehouse for a cup of our favorite blend before dashing off to earn a living, spending time each day on our investments is the *last* thing we want to do.

I have never quite figured out how busy portfolios can somehow produce successful portfolios, but I *have* figured out that the secret to breaking eighty is making my four-foot putts.

As long as Wall Street has a vested interest in lots of transactions and busy portfolios, investors will continue to latch on to the hype and hysteria of Wall Street, perpetuating the misconception that by carefully reviewing market trends, diligently studying mutual fund tables, religiously researching global economies and closely watching interest rates, anyone and everyone can successfully switch in and out of . . .

mid-cap health-care stocks,
emerging market growth funds,
small cap micro-tech stocks
and large cap blue chip funds . . .

and own a successful portfolio.

Hey! Wall Street now offers "mutual fund supermarkets," so investors can not only switch from fund to fund and stock to stock and sector to sector, they can now switch from one *family* of funds to another *family* of funds —

kind-of like one-stop shopping.

And now Wall Street lets investors do all this one-stop shopping with the flick of a switch and the click of a mouse on the Internet.

How totally cool.

There's only one problem.

If the millionaires of this country aren't obsessed with trading their accounts every hour on the hour, who is?

You?

I have a good friend named Marilyn who is too busy juggling her activities as a great mother and successful attorney to design a sector-filled mutual fund account, but she wants to own a successful portfolio for her retirement.

I have a good friend named Bernard who farms and is too busy raising produce for supermarkets to come home at night and shop at a mutual fund supermarket, but he wants to own a successful portfolio for his retirement.

I have a good friend named Margaret who is a physical therapist and is too busy charting progress reports on her computer to trade stocks and mutual funds on the Internet, but she wants to own a successful portfolio for her retirement.

To these three people and millions like them who live life with a passion and purpose and quite frankly couldn't care less about busy portfolios and Wall Street things, congratulations —

you are on your way to becoming successful investors.

For those of us who already ignore Wall Street and are getting on with our lives, the challenge we face in building wealth is to spend a little time learning the difference (and what a difference it is) between busy portfolios and the three fundamental principles of investing.

It doesn't matter whether you have a regular (taxable) account and can choose between 15,000 stocks and funds, or a company-sponsored 401(k) retirement plan that gives you a choice of eight. If you allocate your assets properly, approximate the stock market average and save enough, you maximize your chances of achieving your financial goals.

It's a good idea to learn about these three fundamental principles of investing now because the longer you wait the more painful it becomes, and the last thing you want to do is get caught in the middle of a growing national crisis resulting from too many people reaching retirement age with too little money to sustain themselves — not to mention enjoy themselves.

We've all read the surveys about the average baby boomer who has socked away exactly $26.32 and a few peanut butter sandwiches for her retirement. I suspect those surveys overstate the problem, but not by much.

If the people of this country who work so hard to earn a living continue with their current saving and investing habits, there will be lots of folks who are in for a big surprise when they want to retire, and this surprise won't come in the form of a surprise retirement party. It will come in the form of a dramatically reduced standard of living or a need to prolong their working years at a time in life when the shelf life of a peanut butter sandwich is the last thing they should have to worry about.

Do yourself a big favor. Put this book down, close your eyes and contemplate what your life would be like, today, on 20 percent of your current income.

I would guess that for most people, living on 20 percent of their income would be extremely painful, and if we're honest with ourselves we wouldn't begin to know where to cut and trim so our expenses match an 80 percent reduction in income.

If we slow our lives down just enough to determine whether there *is* a distant financial crisis looming, and then keep our lives slowed down a little longer to learn about the three fundamental principles of investing, it's a crisis that can be easily averted.

There is an enormous benefit to allocating your assets, approximating the stock market average and saving.

It is the benefit of taking control of your financial life so that you, and you alone, are responsible for your actions today and the quality of life when you retire.

When you take control and accept full responsibility for *how your assets are allocated*, you are at the same time letting go of the mistaken belief that the secret to a successful portfolio is to accurately forecast bull and bear markets.

When you take control and accept full responsibility for *approximating the stock market average*, you are at the same time letting go of the mistaken belief that the secret to making money in the stock market is relying on stock market experts.

When you take control and accept full responsibility for *how much you save*, you are at the same time letting go of the mistaken belief that the government safety net will be there to catch you and millions like you when the time comes to retire in style.

A funny thing happens when you begin to take control of one part of your life — whether it is taking control physically, financially or mentally: You gradually notice a positive change in other areas of your life, such as your personal relationships, your performance at work and your ability to embrace your true passions.

Franz Schubert, the great Austrian composer, once said, "I am in this world only for composing."

Wouldn't it be nice to take some of our new-found energy and use it to discover or rediscover a sense of purpose in this world as strong as Franz Schubert's?

The first step in discovering our true passions and talents is to isolate and eliminate clutter in our lives, including in our finances, and a good place to start is to look at how our addiction to clutter is born out of the society we live in.

For instance, if a person is raised in a household that has a habit of watching television four hours a day, there's a good chance that person will become addicted to watching a lot of television.

I am not one to say four hours of television a day is too much television, but there is a little voice inside me that says four hours of television a day will not help me in my journey toward discovering my talents and passions and living a healthy and productive life. Unless people who watch four hours of television a day are creatively shown why watching that much television might be counterproductive to living healthy and productive lives, chances are these people will have a difficult time breaking an addiction to television.

Even though this addiction to television might hinder

someone's ability to think creatively and communicate effectively, watching television is still a difficult habit to break, because for the most part those who are addicted probably don't know any better.

The same is true in investing.

If a person is raised in a society that has a habit of focusing on last year's top mutual funds, this year's hot stocks, and what the Dow Jones Industrial Average did today, eventually this person becomes addicted to the clutter of glossy mutual fund magazines, brokerage firms' recommended buy lists, and high-speed Internet sites, all proclaiming to have the right answers and top funds for you. Unless this person is creatively shown why paying attention to all this financial clutter is counter-productive to one's investment success, he will continue this addiction to Wall Street, all the while ignoring the three most important aspects of investing: asset allocation, approximating the stock market average and saving.

It is a hard addiction to break, because after discussing the weather it seems like everyone wants to talk about cool companies and hot mutual funds, and if you don't own cool companies and hot mutual funds some people might think you are dull and boring.

Don't worry.

It's better to be dull and boring and a successful investor than it is to be loud and obnoxious and unable to retire.

The ironic part of all this dull and boring stuff, if I do say so myself, is that the people who talk only about stocks and bonds are the people who end up being dull and boring. But the people who are embracing life and in their conversations reveal a sense of being immersed in the world at large are the people we enjoy the most.

Come to think of it, that's how this journey got started — meeting up with close friends at a corner coffeehouse in Seattle on rainy Saturday mornings, talking about the week behind us, talking about the week ahead and talking about the kids to be coached, mountains to be climbed and stuff to be done that day.

Those 6:30 A.M. coffeehouse discussions that helped us reconnect with the world after a hectic week usually got started around 6:45, when someone woke up enough to read something in the morning newspaper worth reading, like how bad will traffic get before we finally pass a rapid transit proposal (it passed), or how will the Seattle Mariner's bullpen perform this year (not great) . . . or how much higher can Microsoft go?

The thing I liked most about those 6:30 Saturday morning coffeehouse discussions is that they were over and done with by 7:15, because by 7:15 it was light enough to see through the rain from our corner in the coffeehouse.

And even though we weren't that jazzed to leave our warm coffeehouse corner and go out in the rain to coach kids, climb mountains or get stuff done, we got going anyway, because we learned early on that if you wait for a dry day to do stuff in Seattle it might just never get done.

Looking back on our discussions of soccer games and stock splits, those 6:30 A.M. coffeehouse investors seemed to be the independent types who enjoyed, among other things, the satisfaction of owning successful portfolios. And even though they had fun talking about high-flying stock market issues, these investors understood the importance of diversification, and they also knew that when you take a risk in the stock market you better make sure it's a risk worth taking.

Abraham de Moivre, the French-born mathematician and pioneer in the understanding and application of risk management, never sat with us at our corner coffeehouse table because he died in 1754, but to me he is the ultimate coffeehouse investor. He used to spend his afternoons in an English coffeehouse, selling his knowledge of risk to gamblers, merchants and brokers.

I'm convinced that, were he alive today, Abraham de Moivre would tell us that investing in the stock market to achieve our long-term financial goals is clearly a risk worth taking . . .

relying on Wall Street experts to invest our money in the stock market for us is clearly a risk that is not.

Don't take my word for it, though.

This journey will let you decide for yourself.

Let's get going.

# $\mathscr{2}$ THIS THING CALLED RISK

ONE KEY TO BUILDING A SUCCESSFUL INVESTMENT portfolio is to eliminate the risk you can control and reduce the risk you can't.

One key to living life with a passion and a purpose is to say "yes" to personal risks you can control and embrace the risks you can't.

In looking at ways we can reduce or eliminate this thing called investment risk, let's begin by attempting the impossible, which makes for an exciting journey because it's not very often one gets a chance to attempt the impossible.

I wonder what Sir Edmund Hillary and Tenzing Norgay felt like standing on top of Mount Everest.

I wonder what Roger Bannister felt like running the first sub-four-minute mile.

I wonder what my mother felt like getting eight children ready for early church on Sunday mornings.

If you've never had a chance to attempt the impossible, your wait is over and your time is now. We are about to attempt the impossible of taking a very simple subject — asset allocation — and keeping it simple amidst a financial industry that has a knack for making the subject of asset allocation sound very complicated, very technical, very confusing and very much out of the grasp of anyone who might just happen to possess a little common sense of her own —

which,
I'm assuming,
you do.

Asset allocation simply means dividing up your assets in the right proportions among stocks, bonds and cash to maximize your chance of achieving your financial goal with the minimum amount of investment risk.

Unfortunately, keeping the subject of asset allocation simple is easier said than done because Wall Street has mastered the art of talking out of both sides of its mouth.

I think you know what I mean.

On one side of its mouth, Wall Street whispers about the merits of long-term investing. On the other side of its mouth, Wall Street appeals to our sense of fear and greed by talking about short-term stock market volatility and short-term mutual fund performance.

Just for the heck of it, stand in front of a mirror sometime and try talking out of both sides of your mouth as successfully as the financial industry does. It's not that easy to do.

The problem with Wall Street talking out of both sides of its mouth is that many investors who are tuned in to their own lives and consumed with their own careers are not quite sure what side to listen to — and often end up listening to the side that talks about daily stock market swings and irrelevant mutual fund things.

But then, what can you expect?

That's the loudest side.

It's the side that wants to discuss how your assets should be allocated among capital appreciation funds, blue-chip growth stocks, high-yield bond funds, balanced Latin American utility funds, midcap tech stocks, short-term micro-chip government funds, growth and income balanced funds, emerging market small-cap stocks, large-cap equity funds and medium-term, mortgage-backed, reverse-repo sector funds.

And it should come as no surprise to us that the loudest side is also the side that happens to appeal to our emotions of fear and greed. It isn't easy to keep the subject of asset allocation simple in the midst of a financial industry that tends to appeal to our fear and greed. After all, we don't want to lose money in the stock market (fear). Nor, if we already have a good deal, do we want to miss out on a better deal (greed).

And in an effort to get your business and the fees and expenses that go along with your business, the financial industry can't resist moving from a discussion of long-term investment strategies to conversations about instant account access, next quarter's earnings estimates, on-line hookups, bear markets, standard deviations, daily switching privileges, ten-day moving average trend lines, hourly portfolio valuations, cool Web sites, sector fund rotations and all the other stuff that encourages you to switch the account, send them the money, make the transaction and lock in the fee.

Let's keep in mind that we live in a country where the bottom line is number one, and the financial industry certainly isn't the only industry that is prone to a little fast talking to do what it has to do to make the boss happy.

There are lots of good things that come out of a country that focuses on the bottom line, like a willingness to get the job done because if you don't somebody else will. We need to remember one thing, though. When living in a country in which the bottom line is number one, we are ultimately responsible for our own actions, and if your effort to allocate your assets turns into lots of trades and transactions and your portfolio suffers as a result, you can only blame that person in the mirror.

So let's take responsibility for our own actions and simplify the subject of asset allocation.

Again, asset allocation simply means dividing up your assets in the right proportions among stocks, bonds and cash to maximize your chance of achieving your financial goal with the minimum amount of risk. The critical first step in allocating your assets is to determine what is known as your *investment time horizon*; that is, the years you have left to invest before you start drawing on your investments (which, for most of us, means retirement), and then using your investment time horizon to figure out how to divide up your assets in the right proportions among stocks, bonds and cash.

For example, a twenty-five-year-old with a long investment time horizon needs to make sure that the majority of his assets (80 to 100 percent) are invested in common stocks, which are riskier than bonds or cash in the short-term but prove better investments in the long-term. On the other end of the spectrum, a sixty-four-year-old retiree should consider investing a significant part of her assets (30 to 70 percent) in bonds and/or cash in order to reduce the impact of inevitable stock market declines and to supplement income for living expenses.

How should you allocate your assets? When deciding on the proper mix among asset classes it is important to remember there is no perfect answer. The objective in allocating your assets is to allocate them so your portfolio broadly represents where you are in relation to your investment time horizon.

The sample portfolios in the following charts are simple guidelines to use when allocating your assets amongstocks, bonds and cash, using a retirement age of sixty-five as a yardstick for your investment time horizon.

## Asset Allocation Models

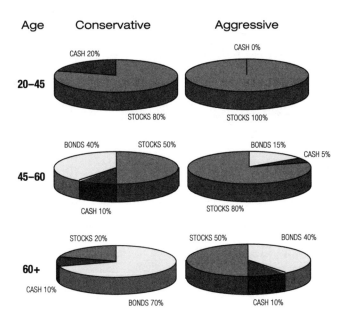

As you can see, even in the most conservative investment portfolio a portion of assets should still be allocated to the stock market to protect the investor from the debilitating impact of inflation.

At the end of each year, review the amount of money you have invested in each class of assets. If a substantial movement in the stock or bond market results in a significant shift away from your desired allocation, you should consider rebalancing your assets to your original allocation percentages, unless, of course you feel comfortable with your current allocation. The following table gives an example of reallocating assets among classes.

| | | |
|---|---|---|
| **ORIGINAL ALLOCATION: $200,000** | 70% IN STOCKS | $140,000 |
| | 25% IN BONDS | $50,000 |
| | 5% IN CASH | $10,000 |
| **AFTER TWO YEARS: $240,400** | STOCKS ARE UP 30% TO . . . | $182,000 |
| | BONDS ARE DOWN 5% TO . . . | $47,500 |
| | CASH IS UP 9% TO . . . | $10,900 |
| | RESULTING IN A YEAR-END TOTAL OF . . . | $240,400 |
| **AT WHICH TIME THE INVESTOR REBALANCES THE YEAR-END TOTAL TO HIS ORIGINAL ALLOCATION** | 70% OF $240,400 IN STOCKS | $168,280 |
| | 25% OF $240,400 IN BONDS | $60,100 |
| | 5% OF $240,400 IN CASH | $12,020 |

Understanding this thing called risk and how it applies to you when allocating your assets is very important, because when it comes to making long-term investment decisions, many of us have a tendency to confuse investment risk with investment opportunity, and we end up allocating too much of our money to investments that are counterproductive to reaching our financial goals based on our investment time horizon.

The first step in understanding this thing called investment risk is to define it — not in the way Wall Street defines it, which make no sense at all —

$$\sigma = \sqrt{\frac{1}{n-1} \cdot \sum_{t=1}^{N} (r_t - \overline{r})^2}$$

but in a way that makes sense in a real world, full of real people doing real jobs and paying for real things, such as college educations, new automobiles and new homes:

*Investment risk is the risk that the money you are counting on to purchase something important or sustain your lifestyle at some point in the future won't be there when you need it.*

There are two major types of investment risk. The first type is *inflation* — the risk of having your living expenses increase faster than the income generated from your investments.

The second type of risk is *stock market volatility* — the risk of losing money in the stock market.

Wall Street doesn't talk much about the first type of risk, inflation, but it does talk a lot about the second type of risk, stock market volatility. Of course. That's the risk that generates lots of trades and transactions.

If we were to take a very scientific survey and call up 10,000 stockbrokers, mutual fund managers and financial analysts and ask them about the risks of investing, I have a sneaking suspicion their perception of investment risk would look something like this . . .

And because the financial industry looks at risk this way, there is a natural tendency for us to look at risk this way.

Instead of looking at investment risk the way Wall Street does, let's look at investment risk based on our investment time horizon.

The chart on page 48 shows the yearly fluctuations of the stock market from 1926 to 1997. As you can see, if you had an investment time horizon of one year or less, there was about a 30 percent chance your stock market money would go down in value during this time period.

Obviously, if you have a one-year investment time horizon and your money is invested in the stock market, you need to weigh the risk of keeping it in the stock market against the importance of having 100 percent of your principle intact one year from now.

The next chart (page 49) shows five-year stock market returns from the same time period. As you can see, when you increase your investment time horizon from one year to five years, your chance of losing money in the stock market drops dramatically.

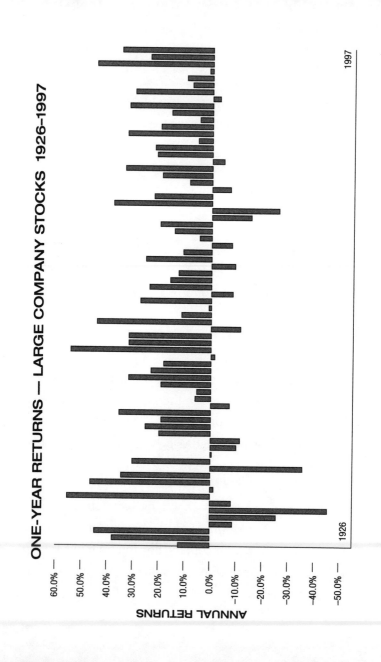

ONE-YEAR RETURNS — LARGE COMPANY STOCKS 1926–1997

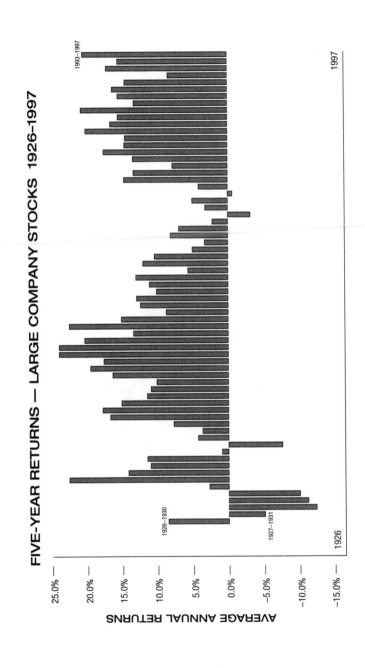

FIVE-YEAR RETURNS — LARGE COMPANY STOCKS 1926–1997

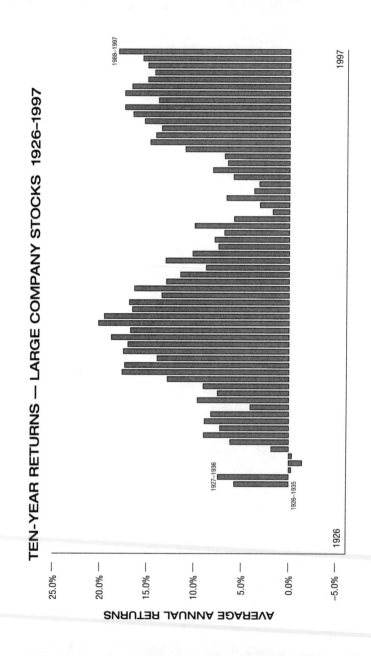

TEN-YEAR RETURNS — LARGE COMPANY STOCKS 1926–1997

The final chart (page 50) shows ten-year stock market returns. As you can see, except for a few ten-year periods following the great crash of 1929, investors never lost money in the stock market!

That's not to say there will never be a ten-year period in which you won't lose money in the stock market. In fact, during any ten-year period *there is a strong probability* you will endure a one- or two-year period in which your stock market investments will decline 20 percent, 30 percent or more. That's the stock market for you. But as you can see, when you have an investment time horizon of ten years or more, an investment in the stock market is clearly a risk worth taking — even if you do have to wait a few more years for the market to bounce back from the inevitable declines in value that happen from time to time.

Even so, I suspect there might be a few investors out there (not to mention the entire financial industry), who are muttering to themselves,

*Hey, wait a minute!*
*Ten years is a long time to stick with something,*
*especially when I am having trouble making it*
*through the week,*

*and every time I turn on the TV*
*or read the newspaper*
*or talk to my neighbor*
*it seems like*
*the Dow*
*is having a cow.*

For those investors with a ten-year investment time horizon who are having trouble making it through a one-week, Wall Street-induced investment time horizon, you might want to make a copy of the ten-year stock market chart and tape it to your bedroom closet door, so that the next time the Dow has a cow you can keep things in perspective and remain committed to your long-term investment strategy.

Because, while Wall Street talks about Dows that have cows, a very unobtrusive word — inflation — continues to eat away at our purchasing power in subtle, subdued ways that quietly blend in with our daily activities of paying for groceries, paying for health care, paying for tuition, paying for automobiles and paying for everything else that goes up in price in amounts too small to merit any attention on the nightly business report when the Dow has a cow and drops 500 points.

And while Wall Street is frantically running around screaming,

"Get a doctor, get a doctor, the Dow is having a cow!"
One year in college has gone from $1,245 to $11,400.
An automobile has gone from $5,817 to $18,563.
A one-day hospital stay has gone from $173 to $952.
A home has gone from $39,400 to $143,090.
The price of a stamp has gone from 4 cents to 33 cents—

(and last I heard they were thinking 34 cents).

Maybe those of us who have a ten-year investment time horizon (or longer) and live in the real world of college educations, automobiles, homes and 33-cent postage stamps should call up those 10,000 Wall Streeters and tell them this is how we view investment risk . . .

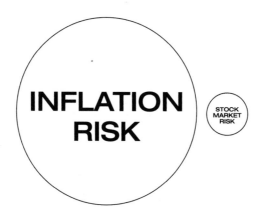

On second thought, don't waste your time.

The easiest way to focus on your long-term investment time horizon and ignore the short-term Wall Street stuff is to ignore the short-term Wall Street stuff.

We all know that the stock market is volatile in the short run because most of us monitor it in the short run. And I am the first to admit that when you follow the stock market on a daily or weekly basis it can be a little nerve-wracking, as indicated by the graph below that shows the movement of the stock market during a three-month period in 1997. This three-month period, if I do say so myself, has an eerie resemblance to a risky mountain-climbing expedition, encouraging even the bravest of long-term investors to stay at home and hide (their money) under a mattress.

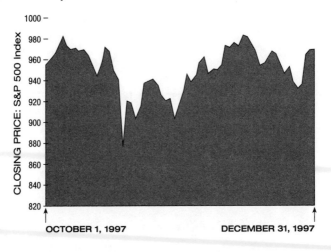

Now compare our risky mountain-climbing chart to the graph below, which simply reflects the long-term (logarithmic) growth of a $1,000 investment from 1926 to 1997.

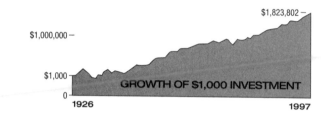

With so many things going on in our lives, we sometimes lose sight of the fact that the three-month period indicated by the risky mountain-climbing chart is the same three-month period that appears as a mere point on the chart of the market's long-term performance.

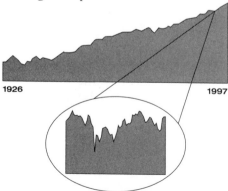

The graph you focus on plays a big part in how you view risk and allocate your assets. Let's face it, if you are addicted to daily stock market swings, there will be times when the short-term volatility in the stock market will make you feel like you are caught hanging on the side of a cliff, and you will be inclined to do things with your investments that are not so smart, like switch mutual funds, trade stocks or move to the sidelines. In reality the smartest thing you can do is direct all your attention to your family, your career and your pursuits, bolstered by an inner confidence that your stock market investments are invested in the chart that doesn't resemble a risky mountain-climbing expedition.

I'm not saying this is an easy task to accomplish, because the financial industry is obsessed with talking about economic avalanches and financial crevasses much more than the price of a postage stamp — and it is only human nature to fear avalanches and crevasses much more than a 4 — er — 33-cent stamp.

For long-term investors who monitor their portfolios four times a year instead of every day, not only is it easier to keep your assets properly allocated, thus minimizing the investment risk that affects you the most — inflation — but by doing so, more of your creative energy is freed up to maximize the personal risks that enrich you the most. Before long, you realize that the personal risks you want to take in life are not that risky. They are an adventure.

The first time I climbed Mt. Rainier was a miserable experience. I climbed with someone who talked too much. I rented my climbing boots and they wore a red hole in my foot. I borrowed a backpack and the strap broke. The stove wouldn't light. It rained.

But we made it to the top.

Looking back on the times I have summitted Mt. Rainier since then (and I have failed many more times than I've succeeded), my favorite ascent was with a man and a woman who were traveling across America one summer after graduating from a college in Virginia — having a good time and sleeping in the back of their truck, stopping in state after state to hike and climb. (Hey, it's great to be young.)

For some crazy reason our climbing party and the two students from Virginia met halfway up Rainier. Two of them and two of us.

There's not much happening halfway up Rainier except that's

where the crevasses start and that's where summertime hikes turn serious, requiring those who want to continue on to get out . . .

their crampons,
seat harnesses,
ice axes,
carabiners,
helmets,
ice screws,
pickets
and ropes.

The two from Virginia had everything except a rope, so we invited them to clip onto our rope and climb with us. You know, the more the merrier.

When climbing Rainier, there is one spot you don't want to dillydally around — the spot on Ingraham Glacier at 11,500 feet that needs to be crossed to get to Disappointment Cleaver — because big blocks of ice have been known to come hurtling down the middle of Ingraham Glacier, causing massive avalanches. And so dillydally we didn't.

At 12,000 feet our two friends from Virginia wanted to turn around. At 13,000 feet they wanted to turn around. At 13,500 feet they wanted to turn around. At 13,501 feet they wanted to turn around. At 14,410 feet we all wanted to turn around, and we did, because we had made it to the top.

Going up Rainier is the easy part, because in the middle of the night the glacier is frozen, the footing is firm and the hot sun hasn't come up yet. Going down is a different story. The sun is hot, you are tired and the glacier is slushy, forcing you to knock slushy snow off your sticky crampons every step of the way. (Clumps of snow on the bottom of your feet are not quite as effective as clean crampons when jumping over a crevasse.)

And when you cross Ingraham Glacier on the way down things can get a little dicey, because the chunks of ice that have been known to come hurtling down the mountain have now had a couple of hours to melt and break free. Fortunately, on this day, the falling chunks of ice were a few minutes early, but not too early that we weren't able to witness an enormous avalanche in front of our eyes.

I suspect the four of us individually reflect on that avalanche from time to time, though I'm not sure because

I've never kept in touch with those two students from Virginia.

Not everyone climbs mountains.

Everyone does encounter risk though, along with the emotional avalanches that are a part of failing and succeeding amidst this thing called life.

Whether it's the risk of presenting a new idea at work in the heat of battle to keep up with the competition, or the risk of recognizing you need to get away from it all and just chill out at your favorite coffeehouse, you only live life once, and you can't let a few emotional avalanches now and then keep you from embracing your dream in pursuit of *your* summit.

I used to chop thistles on our farm with a kid, who, when a plane flew over would look up, wipe his sweaty brow and dream out loud of becoming an airline pilot. As I remember, this simple event of chopping thistles, wiping sweaty brows and dreaming out loud happened several times a day for several years during the hot months of August on a wheat farm in eastern Washington.

This kid did not know the difference between a rudder and a

stabilizer but he did know, in fact he was absolutely positive, he'd rather be piloting an airplane than chopping thistles.

Somewhere today there is an airplane crisscrossing this country copiloted by my kid brother who works for a major airline, and sometimes I wonder what he is dreaming about today.

The journey continues.

## $\mathcal{3}$ APPROXIMATING THE STOCK MARKET AVERAGE

THE PRODUCTIVITY AND GROWTH OF OUR COUNTRY IS simply a reflection of all the brilliant, ingenious, common-sense ideas that are put into action through lots of hard work by you, your friends and your neighbors.

And unless I'm missing something, it seems to me that when we take our hard-earned money and invest it in the stock market, what we are really doing, consciously or unconsciously, is making a commitment to this collective creativity of human beings based on the premise that this unending flow of ideas, combined with our innate desire to improve the quality of life of ourselves and others, will not stop anytime soon.

Unfortunately, Wall Street takes this very simple and very successful approach to investing . . .

and screws it up . . .

by trying to convince us that the secret to our investment success lies in breaking up this collective creativity to invest in specific stocks, industries, trends and mutual funds instead of investing in everything.

It would be one thing if Wall Street were successful in its efforts to beat the entire stock market average by investing in specific stocks, industries, trends and mutual funds. But when Wall Street's efforts to selectively pick and choose continually *underperform* this collective creativity (as reflected by the entire stock market average) and end up costing you hundreds of thousands of dollars in the process, that's where we need to draw the line.

Maybe we should start from Square One.

As you probably know, the annual return of the stock market average is a collective return of *all* the publicly traded companies listed on a particular index, such as the Standard

& Poor's 500 Index or the Wilshire 5000 Index. The good companies as well as the not-so-good companies. Logically, you would think that stock picking "experts," as mutual fund managers claim to be, who spend all day analyzing financial reports, interviewing company presidents, talking to research analysts, reading *The Wall Street Journal* and generally feeling important and intelligent, could pick enough good companies and avoid enough bad companies to outperform the stock market average, which is made up of all the good companies and all the bad companies combined.

They can't.

They don't.

This is Wall Street's best-kept secret, and it's a secret mutual fund managers would rather you didn't know. It's kind-of like hiding a bad report card from your parents.

Now you know.

Only 21 percent of all managed mutual funds beat the stock market average during the last ten-year period.

Only 15 percent of all managed mutual funds beat the stock

market average during the last five-year period.

Only 21 percent of all managed mutual funds beat the stock market average during the last three-year period.

Only 10 percent of all managed mutual funds beat the stock market average in each of the last three-, five- and ten-year periods.[1]

Amazingly, these report cards would be *significantly* worse if the following statistics were included . . .

- the expenses paid on load mutual funds
- the capital gains tax liability of mutual funds held in taxable accounts
- merged or discontinued funds

If I were a mutual fund manager, I'd want to keep this a secret too.

I've had a few bad report cards in my life, including the one from Sister Lucida after telling her that I didn't get much out of her religion class. But I have to say, in my eight years of attending Guardian Angel School, I never had a report card

1. Compared to Wilshire 5000 Index for the period ending March 31, 1999. Compiled using Morningstar's software program Principia™ for Mutual Funds. Used with permission.

quite as ugly as the report cards of mutual fund managers.

If these report cards were handed out by Sister Lucida I suspect most mutual fund managers would be stuck in eighth grade.

Investors who decide to invest their hard-earned money with these underperforming stock-picking experts are destined to underperform the stock market average with them.

It's that simple — and this costly . . .

The following table shows how much underperforming the stock market average costs someone who invests $500 a month over a thirty-year period.

| | UNDERPERFORMING BY THIS AMOUNT | | |
|---|---|---|---|
| YEARS | 2% | 4% | 6% |
| 5 | $2,129 | $4,118 | $5,979 |
| 10 | $12,011 | $22,446 | $31,529 |
| 15 | $38,807 | $70,023 | $95,227 |
| 20 | $100,339 | $174,804 | $230,413 |
| 25 | $230,525 | $387,892 | $496,295 |
| 30 | $492,877 | $801,570 | $997,251 |

*Assumes yearly stock market average of 11 percent*

Not surprisingly, mutual fund managers go to great lengths to hide these bad report cards by drawing our attention away from them and directing it toward performance numbers that have nothing to do with our long-term investment success:

I'M NUMBER ONE!
(For the last three weeks)

I'M NUMBER ONE!
(For risk-adjusted, large-cap mutual funds that begin with the letter x)

I'M NUMBER ONE!
(For Euro-Pacific biotechnology cat food funds)

I'M NUMBER ONE!
(At missing four-foot putts)

Unfortunately, as the report cards reveal, there aren't too many mutual funds that are number one at consistently beating the stock market average.

This phenomenon of underperformance by mutual fund managers is difficult for many investors to accept because many of us have come to depend on experts in many areas of our life, including our stock market investments, and the thought that "professional" stock pickers could collectively do such a lousy job is hard for many investors to comprehend.

For instance, Jim, my dentist, is an expert at taking care of my teeth.

Greg, my mechanic, is an expert at taking care of my car.

Caroline, my doctor, is an expert at keeping me healthy.

In a society that finds comfort in experts, it is only natural to want a "stock-picking expert" to pick stocks for us because investing is a very serious thing, especially when the quality of our retirement depends on it.

I can assure you, if Jim, my dentist, Greg, my mechanic or Caroline, my doctor, had a report card as bad as mutual fund managers I would be in the market for a new dentist, mechanic and doctor, and so would you.

With all due respect to mutual fund managers, who try their hardest and do a very good job at hiding bad report cards, I know of no other industry in which so many self-proclaimed experts try so hard to convince us that they are wildly successful at that which they so miserably fail — out-performing the stock market average.

The problem is that Wall Street is so successful at drawing our attention away from bad report cards, most investors have come to accept this mediocrity, oblivious to any alternatives.

Guess what. *There is an alternative.*

Most of you have probably heard of it by now: approximating the stock market average; that is, coming as close to equaling it as possible.

One way to do this is to invest in a stock index mutual fund. As many of you already know, a stock index fund is simply an unmanaged mutual fund that owns a piece of all the companies of a particular stock market index. The good companies and the not-so-good companies combined.

What a brilliant, ingenious, commonsense idea — that I can't take credit for — but can religiously pass along to those of you who want to unclutter your financial lives and own a sophisticated portfolio. And boy, wouldn't Sister Lucida be proud of me for finally doing something a little religious.

Before we go further, let's discuss the difference between stocks and mutual funds. (It never hurts to review what you probably already know, so here we go.)

When you invest in a common stock, you become part-owner in that company. When you invest in a mutual fund, you indirectly own common stock in many companies. These stocks are all bundled together in one investment called a mutual fund. Managed mutual funds have a person or group of people who call themselves mutual fund managers. Mutual fund managers spend all day trying to make sense out of interest rates, predict future earnings growth, look for undervalued companies and predict overvalued situations, and they do all this with the goal of providing their investors with a rate of return that is better than a specific stock market index. At least I hope that's their goal.

A stock index fund is also a mutual fund, but an *unmanaged* mutual fund. Because it owns a piece of *all* the publicly traded companies that make up a particular stock market index, there is no need for any kind of manager to decide what stocks the fund should invest in. Pretty nifty, eh?

History has shown that an investment in the collective creativity of human beings, as reflected by owning a piece of all the publicly traded companies in an unmanaged stock index mutual fund, is much more profitable over time than an investment with a mutual fund manager who tries to "beat" the stock market average, even though mutual fund managers try with all their might to convince us otherwise.

I suppose that with Wall Street saying "I'm number one" in your ear every day of the year, it is only natural for you to think that the secret to being a successful investor is to *beat* the stock market average with your stock market investments. But by trying to *beat* the stock market average it is easy for investors to ignore the fact that the stock market average itself has historically provided an excellent investment return, and by trying to *beat* an already good thing, you are virtually guaranteed to *end up below it.*

When building and maintaining an investment portfolio, the first step in breaking this addiction to mutual fund managers is to understand why these stock pickers consistently underperform the stock market average. The first reason mutual fund managers consistently underperform the stock market average is because the stock market is already very efficient. In other words, because there are millions and millions of investors out there, if there is a good deal to be had, more often than not somebody has already grabbed it.

For example, if someone scatters seven $1,000 bills next to the Empire State Building, would you call your travel agent and book a flight to New York in the hopes of retrieving a $1,000 bill?

I doubt it.

Why not?

You wouldn't waste your time and money because you would logically conclude that somebody would beat you to the seven $1,000 bills. In picking stocks, as with finding $1,000 bills, once in a while there is a lucky person, but with millions of stock pickers out there, most of the time someone will have beaten a mutual fund manager — or you — to that next underpriced stock.

(For those of you who are caught up in the world of Wall Street things and think it *is* possible for mutual fund managers to consistently find underpriced stocks in a marketplace filled with millions of investors, and you think that the example of the $1,000 bill at the Empire State Building is a little silly, the 90 percent of fund managers who were unable to beat the stock market average in each of the last three-, five- and ten-year periods have done a wonderful job of proving my point.)

The second reason why mutual fund managers consistently underperform the stock market average is because the money they manage is subject to extremely high annual expenses, which reduce your total return.

Quite simply, a $350 plane ticket to New York is too much to pay on the off chance you may find a $1,000 bill.

Mutual fund expenses, buried deep in the middle of every mutual fund prospectus, may seem like a few cents here and a few cents there. Unfortunately, these expenses end up costing investors (yes, even smaller investors) hundreds of thousand of dollars over time, as we will find out in chapter 6. Managed mutual funds have a vested interest in keeping Wall Street's best-kept secret a secret by trying to convince us that picking the good stocks and avoiding the bad stocks is a sophisticated science, better left in the hands of a "stock market expert."

Nothing could be further from the truth.

Even so, I have found that many investors are a little wary at first when introduced to this brilliant, ingenious, commonsense concept of investing in the entire stock market average as represented by an unmanaged stock index mutual fund. Maybe we should see whether there are any other investors out there who embrace this unconventional approach of investing in the entire stock market instead of specific stocks, industries, trends and mutual funds.

Let's check in with some of the largest and most sophisticated investors in our country — the administrators of state pension funds. These people invest billions of dollars and have a fiduciary responsibility to do the right thing for the thousands of state employees who are counting on their state's pension fund when they retire.

First we'll call my home state of Washington and find out how much of its stock market money is indexed in the collective creativity of our country.

What? 100 percent?

No. No. No.

We don't want to know the chance of rain in Seattle on the Fourth of July. We want to know how much of the state pension fund's domestic stock market money is indexed to approximate the stock market average.

100 percent?

No kidding?

Let's check in with the state of California. What? You index 85 percent?

Okay, I admit, out here in the Wild West we tend to be a little off-the-wall. Let's head east and see what other state pension funds are doing.

Kentucky? What? You index 67 percent of your portfolio?

Florida? What? You index 60 percent of your portfolio?

New York? What? You index 75 percent of your portfolio?

Connecticut? What? You index 84 percent of your portfolio? [2]

Hmm. When talking with state administrators, my favorite response was from the administrator of a very large state pension fund of a state that shall remain anonymous (though we Mariner baseball fans don't much care for the pin-striped

2. Based on personal interviews conducted by the author.

uniforms of one of its baseball teams), who said that for long-term investors, "not only is it unreasonable to think they can beat the stock market average, it's probably not doable."

To be honest with you, I can't quite picture the administrator of a state's public pension portfolio going home at night, stopping at the grocery store to pick up some eggs, milk and fruit and then casually throwing into his shopping basket the latest mutual fund magazine from the magazine rack to browse through after dinner in the hopes of picking up a few hot mutual fund ideas for his state's pension fund.

But what the heck, let's say he did.

In February 1994, one of the top mutual fund magazines ran this cover story: *Where to Make Money In '94 — The Best Funds to Buy!* and listed the top eight domestic stock mutual funds to own. Four years later, each of these eight mutual funds had underperformed the stock market average, and collectively they underperformed it by an average of 25 percent annually.

If a state administrator stuck my retirement money in a mutual fund portfolio that underperformed the stock market average by 25 percent annually, I would call him immediately and politely ask him to switch his after-dinner magazine reading material to the *National Geographic.* This is advice your common stock portfolio can do without, unless, of course, you have an uncontrollable urge to underperform the stock market average by 25 percent annually.

Unfortunately, that's how many individual investors make their investment decisions — looking for mutual funds that tout good track records, because track records would seem to be the most logical way to choose a fund, even though it has been shown again and again that past mutual fund performance has little to do with future mutual fund performance. In fact, using past performance numbers as a method for choosing mutual funds is such a lousy idea that mutual fund companies are required by law to tell you it is a lousy idea by listing the following disclaimer in their prospectuses:

*Past performance is no indication of future performance.*

Maybe investors are attracted to past performance numbers because past performance numbers work so well when selecting things like dishwashers.

When it comes our turn to buy a dishwasher, do we go to the appliance store, plunk down a chunk of change, blindly point to a dishwasher in the corner and say, "I'll take that lonely one over there"? No. We do a little research, like maybe asking our friends and neighbors which ones they've liked, and then combine that information with research from something like *Consumer Reports* to find out which dishwasher has performed best in the past and then buy it.

Unfortunately, there is one small problem with using the dishwasher method to select mutual funds.

It doesn't work,

and investors who continue to use the dishwasher method of selecting mutual funds based on past performance numbers are destined to be washing dishes when it comes time to retire.

History has shown it is not such a good idea to invest in mutual funds that have a track record of outperforming the stock market average.

The following three-year, five-year, and ten-year track records suggest you are better off investing at a horse track than in a mutual fund that has at one time or another been a top dog (horse?).

## THREE-YEAR TRACK RECORD

- Mutual funds in the top quartile from 1992 to 1994 collectively under-performed that period's bottom quartile during the next three-year period.

- Mutual funds in the top quartile from 1992 to 1994 dropped on average to 454 out of 750 funds the following three years and under-performed the stock market average by 17 percent annually.

- The top twenty mutual funds from 1992 to 1994 dropped on average to 537 out of 750 funds the following three years and collectively under-performed the stock market average by 26 percent annually.

## FIVE-YEAR TRACK RECORD

- Mutual funds in the top quartile from 1988 to 1992 collectively under-performed that period's bottom quartile during the next five-year period.

- Mutual funds in the top quartile from 1988 to 1992 dropped on average to 278 out of 507 funds the following five years and under-performed the stock market average by 25 percent annually.

- The top twenty mutual funds from 1988 to 1992 dropped on average to 308 out of 507 funds the following five years and collectively under-performed the stock market average by 28 percent annually.

## TEN-YEAR TRACK RECORD

- The top 35 mutual funds from 1978 to 1987 dropped on average to 232 out of 507 funds during the next ten years.
- The top 35 mutual funds from 1978 to 1987 cumulatively under-performed the stock market average by 7 percent annually during the next ten years. [3]

With track records like the ones above, how *should* an investor choose a superior mutual fund? You might be surprised at how easy your choice is. Let's play a quick game called "Outfox the Box."

You are the contestant. There are ten boxes. Each box has some money in it, from $1,000 to $10,000, *and you know how much is in each box.* You get to choose a box, and these are your choices:

| $1,000 | $2,000 | $3,000 | $4,000 | $5,000 |
|--------|--------|--------|--------|---------|
| $6,000 | $7,000 | $8,000 | $9,000 | $10,000 |

(Remember, you know how much is in each box.)

3. Compiled using Morningstar's software program Principia™ for Mutual Funds. 1978-1987 data compiled from *Forbes* magazine's annual mutual fund survey. Used with permission.

Drumroll please . . .

The crowd is screaming.

Your heart is pounding.

Which one will you choose?

This is not a trick question. The answer is obvious. Anyone would choose the $10,000 box. Your decision to choose a mutual fund is just as easy. This time we will change the rules a little. This time, we are going to hide the amounts in the boxes. Except for one box. For this box we reveal that it contains $8,000.

The choices look like this.

| $8,000 | ? | ? | ? | ? |
|--------|---|---|---|---|
| ? | ? | ? | ? | ? |

Now, which box will you choose?

Why?

This answer is also obvious.

You would choose the $8,000 box, because the chance of increasing your winnings is just not worth the risk of choosing an amount substantially less — unless, of course, you are a gambler.

This is not a book on gambling.

This is a book on investing.

There is a big difference.

With the stock market average consistently outperforming 75 to 85 percent of all managed mutual funds, it is a tribute to the massive marketing machine of Wall Street that so many investors spend so much time and effort trying to select the top mutual funds instead of following the lead of state pension fund administrators who have a vested interest in choosing the $8,000 box instead of gambling.

It's important to keep this silly little game in mind when dealing with Wall Street, because Wall Street loves to criticize the concept of indexing as a boring approach to investing in which you forego all opportunity to beat the stock market.

What Wall Street is really saying is,

*"Ignore the $8,000 box and give us your money and we will gladly choose another box for you, because we are self-proclaimed experts at 'outfoxing the box,' and even though the odds are long and the chances are slim that we will succeed, let's give it a try because we love you and your fees."*

Sometimes it takes a silly little game called "Outfox the Box" to break this addiction of always trying to beat the stock market average. It is a hard addiction to break, because the concept of having a *superior* mutual fund by investing in a mutual fund that reflects the stock market *average* is a difficult concept to grasp, especially when thousands of mutual fund managers and thousands of investment advisors and glossy mutual fund magazines are telling you that investing in the stock market average is a mediocre approach to investing in the stock market. Indexing is a case of average being superior, and at first it seems illogical, but, in reality, it's not illogical at all. It's simply common sense.

I frequently encounter this addiction of trying to "Outfox the Box" from friends and investors who tell me they have switched mutual funds several times in the last few years and are still searching for a top-notch mutual fund.

First, I explain to my friends the concept of indexing, which means investing in the entire stock market.

Second, I point out that most mutual funds underperform the stock market average over time.

Next, we review why track records are meaningless when trying to choose a top mutual fund, because the top mutual funds of today tend to underperform the stock market average in the future. And finally, we play a silly little game called "Outfox the Box."

However, most investors are so addicted to relying on past performance numbers, not to mention stock market experts, that I have to start all over.

First, I explain to my friends the concept of indexing, which means investing in the entire stock market.

Second, I point out that most mutual funds underperform the stock market average over time.

Next, we review why track records are meaningless when trying to choose a top mutual fund, because the top mutual funds of today tend to underperform the stock market average in the future. And finally, we play a silly little game called "Outfox the Box."

My favorite response was from a friend of mine who is an environmental scientist and restores parks in San Francisco. For many years, she had been switching from fund to fund, searching for funds that were best for her. One day she called me, looking for a consistent, long-term mutual fund for her portfolio.

First, I explained to her the concept of indexing, which means investing in the entire stock market. Second, I pointed out that most mutual funds underperform the stock market average over time. Next, we reviewed why track records are meaningless when trying to choose a top mutual fund, because the top funds of today tend to underperform the stock market average in the future.

Her response to me was, "I know you like those index funds, but besides that, what is a good fund to invest in?"

So we started all over.

First, I explained to her the concept of indexing, which means investing in the entire stock market. Second, I pointed out that most mutual funds underperform the stock market average over time. Next, we reviewed why track records are meaningless when trying to choose a top mutual fund, because the top funds of today tend to underperform the stock market average in the future, and finally we played a game of "Outfox the Box."

Suddenly, a lightbulb went on. Her exact reply to me was, "Why would anyone consider anything but indexing?"

At that moment, my friend from San Francisco freed herself from the clutter of Wall Street, which is a big load off her shoulders because she is one person who would rather spend her time restoring parks in San Francisco than sorting through 8,000 mutual funds and 7,000 stocks every other year in an effort to build and maintain her common stock portfolio.

Oh, by the way, I hope you enjoy the parks the next time you are in San Francisco.

# *4* BUILDING A COMMON STOCK PORTFOLIO

ONCE YOU REMOVE YOURSELF FROM WALL STREET'S complete and total obsession with trying to *beat* the stock market average and accept the fact that *approximating* the stock market average is a rather sophisticated approach to the whole thing, building a successful common stock portfolio becomes an immensely gratifying experience.

Especially when you relax and remember that you are building a common stock portfolio, not a space shuttle.

This is important, because even though we all have that innate creativity that yearns to build something and watch it grow — whether it be a project at work, a child or a garden

— we also have a tendency to throw up our hands in despair and call in the experts when faced with a task that those same experts have labeled "too complicated for you."

Building a common stock portfolio can be summed up in one word: diversify, diversify, diversify.

Okay, three words.

Diversification simply means making sure your stock market investments are aligned with the collective creativity of our country and are not subject to the more volatile ups and downs of specific stocks, industries, trends or business cycles. That's not to say fortunes haven't been made in one-stock portfolios, because they have. Just ask Bill.

No, not me.
The other Bill.

It is probably very exciting to have your entire portfolio invested in one stock that goes up and up forever, although I wouldn't know because it has never happened to me. But the reward of owning a one-stock portfolio needs to be weighed against the risk of having that same one-stock portfolio go down and down forever as you approach retirement.

The more your portfolio is diversified in many different companies in many different industries, the less your financial goal is dependent on you or anyone else's ability to successfully pick individual stocks, industries or trends — something mutual fund managers have proven is not easily done.

That's why indexing your portfolio makes so much sense. Not only does it give you the ultimate in diversification by owning the widest selection of companies in the maximum number of industries, but it simplifies your selection process of narrowing down 8,000 funds and 7,000 stocks to a couple of sensible mutual funds.

The simplest approach to diversifying your stock market investments is to invest in *one* index fund that represents the entire stock market. The problem with having your entire common stock portfolio invested in one "entire-stock-market" index fund is that eventually, at some backyard barbecue, you will cross paths with a Wall Streeter who, upon learning that your entire portfolio consists of *only one mutual fund,* will argue that you are way underdiversified and will pay for that mistake the next time the stock market drops.

Just smile and say please pass the potato salad.

HOWEVER . . . even though an entire-stock-market index fund is a simple, smart way to invest — especially for those who currently have twelve different mutual funds and eight different stock positions and no earthly idea how these investments are performing, much less how they all fit together — we *can* combine this thing called diversification with our index-fund approach and divide our stock holdings among three groups:

large company stocks,
small company stocks
and international stocks

and build a common stock portfolio using three index funds that represent each of these three groups of common stocks.

The advantage to investing in three separate index funds instead of one entire-stock-market index fund is that it takes this diversification thing one step further by introducing international stocks into your portfolio. And it allows you to construct a personalized portfolio to match your temperament and investment time horizon.

For instance, investors who have a longer time horizon and are able emotionally to accept increased volatility can add to their holdings in small cap and international stock groups and thus provide themselves with an opportunity for increased returns over time beyond what large company stocks offer. But for investors with a more conservative demeanor, or those who are nearing a financial goal, owning more large company stocks should be considered, as these stocks have traditionally been much less volatile than international or small company stocks and have provided more income from dividends.

The following illustrates two portfolio approaches to diversifying among three groups of index funds.

## AGGRESSIVE PORTFOLIO

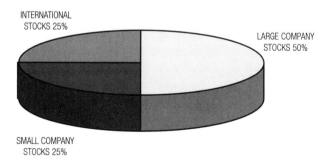

INTERNATIONAL
STOCKS 25%

LARGE COMPANY
STOCKS 50%

SMALL COMPANY
STOCKS 25%

## CONSERVATIVE PORTFOLIO

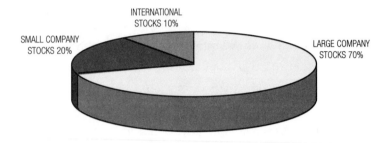

INTERNATIONAL STOCKS 10%

SMALL COMPANY STOCKS 20%

LARGE COMPANY STOCKS 70%

In addition to choosing a three-index-fund approach, you can take this thing called diversification one step further by breaking the large company and small company stocks into two components — value and growth — and building an indexed portfolio utilizing these two subgroups. Instead of owning three index funds, your common stock portfolio would now consist of five index funds:

large company growth,
large company value,
small company growth,
small company value
and international.

Keep in mind that if you choose to add value and growth index funds to your portfolio, you are doing nothing more than fine-tuning an already good thing. It simply takes this thing we're talking about — diversification — one (small) step further. (For help in selecting index funds among these five groups, turn to the Appendix, which lists index funds by categories.)

In chapter 2 we learned the importance of annually rebalancing your investment portfolio among stocks, bonds and cash to make sure your investments are in line with the type (and amount) of investment risk you want to maintain. The same rebalancing concept holds true for the common stock portion of your portfolio. Whether the common stock portion of your portfolio is aggressive or conservative, the most important factor when diversifying is to adhere to this asset allocation strategy, because when you stick to your strategy and rebalance your assets at year-end, buy and sell decisions are no longer arbitrary but are instead objectively carried out according to your predetermined plan. The result: A portfolio that has less volatility without sacrificing performance.

Let's look at an example of rebalancing a common stock portfolio at year-end with an investor who makes an initial investment of $40,000.

| | | |
|---|---|---|
| **ORIGINAL ALLOCATION: $40,000** | 60% LARGE COMPANY INDEX FUND | $24,000 |
| | 25% SMALL COMPANY INDEX FUND | $10,000 |
| | 15% INTERNATIONAL INDEX FUND | $6,000 |
| **AFTER ONE YEAR: $43,400** | LARGE COMPANIES ARE UP 12% TO ... | $26,880 |
| | SMALL COMPANIES ARE UP 7% TO ... | $10,700 |
| | INTERNATIONAL ARE DOWN 3% TO ... | $5,820 |
| | RESULTING IN A YEAR-END TOTAL OF ... | $43,400 |
| **AT WHICH TIME THE INVESTOR REBALANCES THE YEAR-END TOTAL TO HER ORIGINAL ALLOCATION** | 60% OF $43,400 IN THE LARGE COMPANY INDEX FUND | $26,040 |
| | 25% OF $43,400 IN THE SMALL COMAPNY INDEX FUND | $10,850 |
| | 15% OF 43,400 IN THE INTERNATIONAL INDEX FUND | $6,510 |

Sometimes it is emotionally difficult to reallocate assets away from the class that is doing well (in this case, large company stocks) and invest them in the class that has underperformed. But those who neglect this important aspect of portfolio diversification often find that when the tide eventually turns (as it always does), they are stuck with an excessively large, underperforming asset class.

It's easy to rebalance a portfolio in a tax-deferred retirement account because you are not subject to a capital gains tax on profits taken. This means you can sell stock as part of your rebalancing plan and not have to pay taxes on any profits from that sale — those profits are reinvested within your tax-deferred account.

If instead you have a regular (taxable) account, you need to consider the impact a capital gains tax will have on your rebalancing efforts. In this case, instead of selling and buying to rebalance your account as we did in the above example (again, because selling stock in a taxable account results in capital gains taxes), it might make sense to leave existing money where it is and direct *new* money into that portion of your portfolio that is underrepresented according to your desired allocation strategy. Before you make any portfolio changes that could result in a significant tax liability, it's always best to consult with your accountant or tax attorney.

The task of building an indexed common stock portfolio is pretty straightforward. Unfortunately, many qualified retirement plans, including 401(k)s, do not include index funds. For those investors whose only investment in common stocks is through retirement plans that do not include index funds, their choices are not as simple.

In my opinion, any company that doesn't provide employees an opportunity to index their retirement savings in the three distinct common stock groups should be held accountable to their employees to the extent that the company plan's managed mutual funds underperform their respective stock market indices.

Plan A for solving this problem is to go to your employers and encourage them to include index funds in their choice of funds (which some companies already do). If they balk, politely ask whether they would be willing to make up the difference to the extent that the managed mutual funds underperform their respective benchmark indices.

If Plan A fails or if you hesitate to share a little common sense with your employer, try Plan B: Anonymously give your employer a copy of this book and highlight this chapter.

If your employer thinks indexing a retirement account is a far-fetched idea, tell your employer that indexing is the pre-ferred method of investing for the very large and sophisti-cated public pension plans that have a fiduciary responsi-bility to do the right thing in providing for their employees at retirement, and you were wondering whether they also had the same type of commitment.

If Plan A fails and Plan B fails, try Plan C:

Make lemonade out of lemons.

That is, continue to focus on the goal of approximating the stock market average with the managed mutual funds you have chosen from your company's plan by not switching them, trading them or swapping them for something else — except when you rebalance your investment portfolio every year-end.

If you need help figuring out which of your plan's funds fall into which categories (large cap, small cap and international), ask your benefits coordinator or mutual fund company to help you. If you find out that your retirement plan has ten large company funds, six small company funds and four international funds, it is not necessary to own all twenty funds. Choose one or two from each group and then stick with them. If your funds begin to underperform the other funds in the same group *don't worry about it*, because once you switch to another fund, you have fallen into the trap of using the dishwasher method of choosing mutual funds, which we found out in the last chapter doesn't work.

Instead of comparing your current funds to other, better-performing funds, you should compare your current funds to their appropriate stock market indices. For instance, if your fund is a large company fund, you should compare its performance to a large company index. If your fund is a small company fund, compare it to a small company index. Benchmark indices can be found in the stock market summary on the front page of section C in *The Wall Street Journal*.

## STOCK MARKET SUMMARY

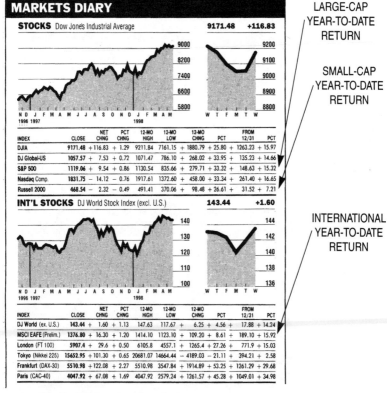

### MARKETS DIARY

**STOCKS**  Dow Jones Industrial Average          9171.48    +116.83

| INDEX | CLOSE | NET CHNG | PCT CHNG | 12-MO HIGH | 12-MO LOW | 12-MO CHNG | PCT | FROM 12/31 | PCT |
|---|---|---|---|---|---|---|---|---|---|
| DJIA | 9171.48 | + 116.83 | + 1.29 | 9211.84 | 7161.15 | + 1880.79 | + 25.80 | + 1263.23 | + 15.97 |
| DJ Global-US | 1057.57 | + 7.53 | + 0.72 | 1071.47 | 786.10 | + 268.02 | + 33.95 | + 135.23 | + 14.66 |
| S&P 500 | 1119.06 | + 9.54 | + 0.86 | 1130.54 | 835.66 | + 279.71 | + 33.32 | + 148.63 | + 15.32 |
| Nasdaq Comp. | 1831.75 | − 14.12 | − 0.76 | 1917.61 | 1372.60 | + 458.00 | + 33.34 | + 261.40 | + 16.65 |
| Russell 2000 | 468.54 | − 2.32 | − 0.49 | 491.41 | 370.06 | + 98.48 | + 26.61 | + 31.52 | + 7.21 |

**INT'L STOCKS**  DJ World Stock Index (excl. U.S.)          143.44    +1.60

| INDEX | CLOSE | NET CHNG | PCT CHNG | 12-MO HIGH | 12-MO LOW | 12-MO CHNG | PCT | FROM 12/31 | PCT |
|---|---|---|---|---|---|---|---|---|---|
| DJ World (ex. U.S.) | 143.44 | + 1.60 | + 1.13 | 147.63 | 117.67 | + 6.25 | + 4.56 | + 17.88 | + 14.24 |
| MSCI EAFE (Prelim.) | 1376.80 | + 16.30 | + 1.20 | 1414.10 | 1123.10 | + 109.20 | + 8.61 | + 189.10 | + 15.92 |
| London (FT 100) | 5907.4 | + 29.6 | + 0.50 | 6105.8 | 4557.1 | + 1265.4 | + 27.26 | + 771.9 | + 15.03 |
| Tokyo (Nikkei 225) | 15652.95 | + 101.30 | + 0.65 | 20681.07 | 14664.44 | − 4189.03 | − 21.11 | + 394.21 | + 2.58 |
| Frankfurt (DAX-30) | 5510.98 | + 122.08 | + 2.27 | 5510.98 | 3547.84 | + 1914.89 | + 53.25 | + 1261.29 | + 29.68 |
| Paris (CAC-40) | 4047.92 | + 67.08 | + 1.69 | 4047.92 | 2579.24 | + 1261.57 | + 45.28 | + 1049.01 | + 34.98 |

LARGE-CAP YEAR-TO-DATE RETURN

SMALL-CAP YEAR-TO-DATE RETURN

INTERNATIONAL YEAR-TO-DATE RETURN

*From* The Wall Street Journal. *Used with permission.*

Remember, if you invest in more than two actively managed mutual funds in each of the three common stock groups you are making your investment journey unnecessarily cluttered.

Diversification and making sure you come as close as you can to approximating  the stock market average are what building a common stock portfolio is all about. Unfortunately, the ease with which you are able to access your account through tools such as telephone switching privileges and Internet trading might lead you to believe that your stock market success is based on your ability to quickly and cleverly move among top funds and hot stocks.

This switch-to-get-rich mentality that is so pervasive in the investment world is absolutely disastrous for someone who is serious about building and maintaining a successful common stock portfolio.

What I just said is so important to your investment success I will repeat it.

This switch-to-get-rich mentality that is so pervasive in the investment world is absolutely disastrous for someone who is serious about building and maintaining a successful common stock portfolio. [1]

We're not quite finished.

In addition to investing in mutual funds in a qualified retirement account, many employees who work for publicly traded companies are also given the opportunity to invest some of their retirement money in company stock. If you think you are working for a good company, then it is a good idea to own some of that company. But be careful. Too much of a good thing can turn out to be a bad thing.

I know, because I like ice cream.

There are countless instances in which great companies have experienced declines of 40, 50, 60 percent or more in the price of their stock for no explainable reason, even when the stock market as a whole has gone up in value. If you feel confident in your ability to predict the inexplicable and are willing to risk a substantial amount of your retirement assets on this ability, then who am I to caution otherwise.

If you prefer a successful diversified investment strategy instead with the money you are counting on to live on when

1. According to Dalbar, Inc., the average equity mutual fund investor switches funds every three years and has captured only one-fifth of the stock market appreciation for the fourteen-year period ending December 31, 1997. Used with permission.

you retire, don't allocate more than 10 to 20 percent of your retirement money to your company's common stock, and don't forget to reallocate your company stock in the same way you reallocate your other assets at the end of each year.

Enough said.

Let's talk about food — my favorite subject.

## $5$   MY FAVORITE PIECE OF PIE

I CAN'T WAIT TO TALK ABOUT FOOD, BECAUSE IF YOU ask me, using your creative energies in the kitchen is a lot more fun (and productive) than trying to figure out which way the stock market is headed. And wouldn't you know it, the more time you spend on fun and productive things (like baking pies, my specialty), the less time you spend worrying about hot stocks and cool mutual funds.

This is important, because if you are a long-term investor and you are constantly worrying about hot stocks and mutual funds, you are ignoring the biggest piece of the investment pie — *compounding* — and it is a piece of the pie you can't afford to ignore.

From 1978 to 1997, a $10,000 investment in the stock market average would have grown, with dividends reinvested, to $215,861. Of that $205,861 increase, 46 percent was due to the price of the underlying common stocks going up in price, *and 54 percent was due to the reinvestment of dividends.*

## IMPACT OF DIVIDEND REINVESTMENT
## S&P 500 INDEX 1978 TO 1997

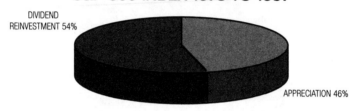

DIVIDEND
REINVESTMENT 54%

APPRECIATION 46%

A little background: Most companies pay out some of their profits each quarter to their shareholders — a dividend. Recipients have the option of taking this dividend check, cashing it and spending it, or reinvesting it; that is, buying more shares of a particular stock or mutual fund. This is called dividend reinvestment.

When we reinvest our dividends instead of spending them, we are able to earn dividends on our original dividends. Ideally, we turn around and reinvest those dividends in order to earn even *more* dividends. All this stuff of earning dividends off dividends off dividends off dividends is called compounding. Most companies increase their dividends each year, so, as an added bonus, the money you compound is constantly increasing.

Albert Einstein, a pretty bright guy, once said something to the effect that "the eighth wonder of the world is the powerful effect that compounding has on your money."

I shared this largest piece-of-pie story once with a friend of mine who replied, "Yeah, but the smallest piece of the pie is where all the action's at."

So, for everyone interested in "action," you can skip the rest of this chapter.

But for those who want to build wealth, ignore Wall Street and get on with their lives, you might find the subject of compounding compelling, even though it means letting your investments just sit there and compound

and compound
and compound.

Let's look at this from a different angle.

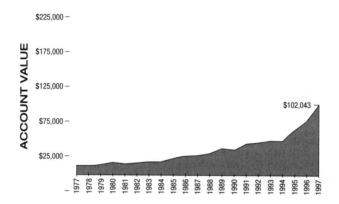

The above graph shows how a $10,000 investment in the stock market grew over a twenty-year period when the investor took all the dividends in cash. The graph below shows how this same $10,000 investment grew when the dividends were reinvested.

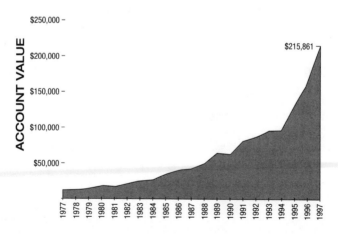

Big difference, huh?

The nice thing about owning a stock index mutual fund, or any other mutual fund for that matter, is that you can elect to have all of your dividends automatically reinvested.

Investors who spend time selling stocks and mutual funds that go up in price are missing out on the largest piece of the money pie because they don't give their investments a chance to sit there and do what they are supposed to do — compound. If you own stocks or mutual funds and reinvest the dividends, your money is put to work in the biggest piece of pie, and the time you save by not obsessing over buy low and sell high strategies can be used to pursue those things in your life you really have fun at . . .

like baking pies.

Speaking of pies, people who bake pies have a blood pressure level one-third lower than that of society at large.

According to me.

When you bake a pie, you can't help but smile and feel in harmony with the world. My favorite pie is pumpkin pie. It tastes great and is less filling. You know you're off to a good start when you read the ingredients in a can of pumpkin: pumpkin.

No monosodium glutamates.
No thiamine mononitrates.
No sodium tripolysphosphates.
No bitasium phosphate.

Just pumpkin.

Here's all the stuff you need:

> 1 (16 ounce) can solid pack pumpkin
> 1 egg
> 1 teaspoon cinnamon
> 1 teaspoon pumpkin pie spice
> 1 (12 ounce) can evaporated milk
> 1 9-inch pie shell

Preheat the oven to 425°F. Dump all the above stuff (except the pie shell) into a bowl and stir it up and then dump all the stirred-up stuff into the pie shell and stick it in the oven. (Please note: If you use a metal pie dish, bake the pie with a cookie sheet underneath so the bottom of the pie shell doesn't burn.) After 15 minutes, reduce the heat to 350°F. Bake for about 40 or 50 minutes. Stick a knife in it, and if it comes out clean, you're done.

You can now show your friends and family the powerful impact that dividend reinvestment has on your very own pumpkin pie!

I love this pie stuff, but we must be moving on.

# *6* LIFE, LOGIC AND PARADOXES

LET'S TALK A LITTLE BIT ABOUT LIFE, LOGIC, LEARN-
ing, investing and paradoxes.

Paradox is one of those words we are 95 percent sure we
know the meaning of but check the dictionary anyway. I'll
save you the trouble.

**par•a•dox** (par´ə-doks) n.1. a seemingly contradictory
statement that may nonetheless be true.[1]

Before we talk about the greatest investment paradox of all
time, let's talk a little about life, logic and learning.

1. *The American Heritage Dictionary* (Boston, Ma: Houghton Mifflin Co., 1976.)

In our journey through life, I think we can logically say that the more we learn, the better off we are. This observation fits neatly into the way we conduct our affairs, live our lives and survive in this world. Whether it is learning a new subject in first grade, revamping a production line problem or becoming a better parent, the more we learn, the better off we are.

However, when it comes to investing, you can *kiss this logic good-bye*, because the less time you spend trying to learn everything there is to know about stocks, bonds and mutual funds, the better off you are. But you do need to know a few things, including how expenses and taxes affect your portfolio, and the lesson to learn is:

The less you pay in expenses and taxes, the better off you are.

There you go. Class dismissed.

The *second-greatest investment paradox of all time* is that so many seemingly sophisticated mutual fund managers stick you with expenses and taxes year after year in the process of consistently underperforming the stock market average.

The *greatest investment paradox of all time* is that so many seemingly sophisticated investors continue to give these mutual fund managers bundles of money to do it again next year. By the time most investors realize what's going on, it's usually too late.

When you pay a mutual fund manager a few cents here and a few cents there in the form of annual operating expenses, and you pay the U.S. government a few cents here and a few cents there in the form of capital gains taxes resulting from all the trades done by your mutual fund manager, eventually a few cents here and a few cents there add up to thousands and thousands and hundreds of thousands of dollars, even in smaller accounts.

Good money.

Gone from your account forever.

It seems to me that we are so darned busy attending our children's activities, trying to squeeze in a vacation and working on Saturdays that we rarely (if ever) take time to figure out how expenses and taxes impact our investments over time. Eventually, instead of having thousands and thousands and hundreds of thousands of additional dollars at retirement to do the things we have always wanted to do, like put a down payment on a lake cabin, take an oil painting class, buy a motorcycle, travel with children and grandchildren, start a new business or pay bills, we have paid thousands and thousands and hundreds of thousands of dollars to a mutual fund manager and the U.S. government in expenses and taxes.

That's not good.

I am not saying that an investor's main goal should be to avoid all expenses and taxes. I am simply showing you how excessive expenses and taxes impact a portfolio. You can take it from there.

Before reviewing the impact of a managed mutual fund's annual expenses, let me clarify one thing: Every mutual fund — including any unmanaged stock index fund — has annual expenses. I bring this to your attention only because, on more than one occasion, I have asked mutual fund investors what their funds' annual expenses are and they reply, "I own a no load. I don't have annual expenses."

They are wrong.

"No load" means no one-time commission on your mutual fund. "No load" does not mean you don't pay an annual mutual fund expense, because you do. If you don't believe me, look it up in your mutual fund's prospectus.

It doesn't matter what kind of mutual fund you own — no loads, front loads, back loads, side loads, top loads or bottom loads — every mutual fund charges an annual expense. They don't send you a bill every month like your utility company does, but believe me, you pay it. Mutual fund companies simply collect their fee by reducing your price per share.

Maybe if mutual fund companies sent a bill each month, more investors would take the time to see whether they were getting their money's worth.

The easiest way to find out your mutual fund's annual expense is to call the company and ask them. Or, better yet, look in your mutual fund's prospectus for a fee table, sometimes called an expenses table.

It will look something like this:

---

**ANNUAL FUND OPERATING EXPENSES**
(as a percentage of average net assets)

| | |
|---|---|
| MANAGEMENT FEE | 1.00% |
| 12b-1 FEES | 0.25% |
| OTHER EXPENSES | 0.25% |
| TOTAL MUTUAL FUND EXPENSE | 1.50% |

---

The average expense ratio for a managed stock mutual fund is 1.54 percent of your money.[2] You can build an indexed portfolio for .25 percent of your money.[3] Without overstating the obvious, that's about 80 percent less (not to mention that with an indexed mutual fund, you are also assured of at least approximating the stock market average).

I wonder whether one of the reasons so few investors pay attention to annual mutual fund expenses is because annual mutual fund expenses are quoted in warm and fuzzy numbers like 1 and 2 percent instead of enormously large numbers like $315,423.

Let's look at how annual mutual fund expenses affect you, not in warm and fuzzy numbers of 1 and 2 percent, but in

---

2. Compiled using Morningstar's software program Principia™ for Mutual Funds. Used with permission.
3. Even though some index fund expense ratios are higher, many index funds charge .25 percent or less. There is no need to pay more.

numbers that most of us relate to — cold cash — because
it's the cold cash of enormously large numbers, not warm
and fuzzy percentages, that will be missing from our portfolios when we need it most.

Below is a table that shows the cold-cash impact that annual expenses have on a managed mutual fund compared to
an unmanaged stock index fund over a fifteen-year period.

| End of year | Value of managed mutual fund with fees of 1.5% | Value of stock index fund with fees of .25% | Difference |
|---|---|---|---|
| 1 | $6,317 | $6,361 | $43 |
| 2 | $13,262 | $13,440 | $177 |
| 3 | $20,897 | $21,320 | $423 |
| 4 | $29,288 | $30,089 | $800 |
| 5 | $38,513 | $39,849 | $1,335 |
| 6 | $48,653 | $50,711 | $2,057 |
| 7 | $59,800 | $62,801 | $3,000 |
| 8 | $72,053 | $76,256 | $4,202 |
| 9 | $85,522 | $91,231 | $5,708 |
| 10 | $100,328 | $107,897 | $7,569 |
| 11 | $116,603 | $126,446 | $9,843 |
| 12 | $134,494 | $147,090 | $12,596 |
| 13 | $154,160 | $170,067 | $15,906 |
| 14 | $175,778 | $195,638 | $19,860 |
| 15 | $199,541 | $224,098 | $24,557 |

*$500 monthly investment, assuming 11 percent annual return*

Even though managed mutual funds as a whole have underperformed the stock market average by 15 percent during the fifteen-year period ending December 31, 1997, let's give managed mutual funds a break they don't deserve and assume that the average fund *equaled* the stock market average, prior to subtracting annual operating expenses, so we can isolate the impact of expenses on your fund.

You don't need to spend all day Saturday and half of Sunday poring over glossy mutual fund magazines to figure out which fund — a managed fund or an unmanaged index fund — has a leg up or down when it comes to annual mutual fund expenses.

It gets worse.

For younger investors who know that they might have an investment time horizon a little longer than fifteen years, the table on the next page shows the impact that annual mutual fund expenses have over a thirty-year period.

At first glance, annual operating expenses hidden deep in the middle of every mutual fund prospectus might seem like mere pocket change.

| End of year | Value of managed mutual fund with fees of 1.5% | Value of stock index fund with fees of .25% | Difference |
|---|---|---|---|
| 16 | $225,664 | $255,774 | $30,110 |
| 17 | $254,378 | $291,026 | $36,648 |
| 18 | $285,942 | $330,261 | $44,319 |
| 19 | $320,639 | $373,928 | $53,289 |
| 20 | $358,780 | $422,527 | $63,748 |
| 21 | $400,706 | $476,616 | $75,911 |
| 22 | $446,793 | $536,815 | $90,022 |
| 23 | $497,454 | $603,814 | $106,360 |
| 24 | $553,143 | $678,380 | $125,238 |
| 25 | $614,359 | $761,370 | $147,011 |
| 26 | $681,650 | $853,734 | $172,084 |
| 27 | $755,620 | $956,531 | $200,911 |
| 28 | $836,931 | $1,070,940 | $234,009 |
| 29 | $926,313 | $1,198,273 | $271,960 |
| 30 | $1,024,565 | $1,339,988 | $315,423 |

*$500 monthly investment, assuming 11 percent annual return*

To anyone who thinks $315,423 is mere pocket change, I'd like to have your pockets.

Investing in a managed mutual fund is no laughing matter, unless you are a mutual fund manager, then you get to laugh all the way to the bank.

Mutual fund managers are paid an average salary of

$475,700[4] to consistently underperform the stock market average. The sad part is, the money you pay them to underperform the stock market average comes out of your retirement money. It's just that most investors are too busy to stop and calculate that $315,423 of their retirement money might be a little too much to pay someone to consistently underperform the stock market average.

Now for the scary part. In addition to annual mutual fund expenses, many investors also pay a financial advisor or stockbroker an annual management fee of 1 to 2.5 percent to select and then watch over their managed mutual funds.

I am not an expert in advanced trigonometry, but I am smart enough to figure out that when annual mutual fund expenses of .75 to 2 percent are combined with yearly advisory fees of 1 to 2 percent, many investors end up paying 2 to 3 percent of the total value of their portfolio in yearly expenses and fees.

*When the stock market is returning 26 percent a year it's easy to swallow 2 to 3 percent in expenses and fees. But when the stock market returns 11 to 12 percent a year (its historical average), 2 to 3 percent in expenses and fees eats up one-fourth of your investment earnings.*

4. Average figure, with a range of $150,000 to $1,000,000+. Buck Consultants, 1997. Used with permission.

I am not one to pass judgment, because if the financial industry can charge its customers 2 to 3 percent and get away with it, then let the good times roll. But if you want my humble opinion on the matter, giving up one-fourth of our investment earnings each year in expenses and fees for something most of us can do better ourselves flat-out doesn't make sense. Below is a table that summarizes the impact of 2.5 percent in combined mutual fund expenses and advisory management fees over a fifteen-year period.

| End of year | Value of managed portfolio with fees of 2.5% | Value of stock index fund with fees of .25% | Difference |
|---|---|---|---|
| 1 | $6,284 | $6,361 | $78 |
| 2 | $13,123 | $13,441 | $318 |
| 3 | $20,566 | $21,320 | $754 |
| 4 | $28,667 | $30,090 | $1,422 |
| 5 | $37,485 | $39,849 | $2,365 |
| 6 | $47,082 | $50,712 | $3,630 |
| 7 | $57,527 | $62,801 | $5,274 |
| 8 | $68,895 | $76,256 | $7,361 |
| 9 | $81,269 | $91,231 | $9,963 |
| 10 | $94,736 | $107,898 | $13,162 |
| 11 | $109,393 | $126,447 | $17,054 |
| 12 | $125,346 | $147,091 | $21,745 |
| 13 | $142,709 | $170,067 | $27,358 |
| 14 | $161,606 | $195,639 | $34,032 |
| 15 | $182,175 | $224,099 | $41,924 |

*$500 monthly investment, assuming 11 percent annual return*

Now let's look at the thirty-year investment chart that shows the impact of management expenses and advisory fees.

When making investment decisions today that will impact your long-term financial goals of tomorrow, it's tempting to focus on the latest, hottest, handsomest mutual fund manager profiled in your Sunday newspaper's business section. Maybe, instead, we should begin to focus on the $508,789 in cold cash that will be missing from our portfolios when we retire.

| End of year | Value of managed portfolio with fees of 2.5% | Value of stock index fund with fees of .25% | Difference |
|---|---|---|---|
| 16 | $204,561 | $255,744 | $51,213 |
| 17 | $228,925 | $291,026 | $62,101 |
| 18 | $255,444 | $330,261 | $74,817 |
| 19 | $284,306 | $373,928 | $89,622 |
| 20 | $315,720 | $422,527 | $106,807 |
| 21 | $349,910 | $476,616 | $126,706 |
| 22 | $387,123 | $536,815 | $149,692 |
| 23 | $427,625 | $603,814 | $176,189 |
| 24 | $471,706 | $678,380 | $206,674 |
| 25 | $519,684 | $761,370 | $241,686 |
| 26 | $571,903 | $853,734 | $281,831 |
| 27 | $628,738 | $956,531 | $327,793 |
| 28 | $690,596 | $1,070,940 | $380,344 |
| 29 | $757,922 | $1,198,273 | $440,351 |
| 30 | $831,199 | $1,339,988 | $508,789 |

*$500 monthly investment, assuming 11 percent annual return*

And don't forget, these hypothetical examples assume your financial advisor was able to choose for you a managed mutual fund portfolio that approximated the stock market average prior to subtracting expenses and fees.

That, my friend, is an awfully big assumption.

Which brings me to my next point, and for investors who have a desire to work with a financial advisor anyway, you need to pay close attention. In chapters 3 and 4 we discovered how to successfully build and maintain a diversified common stock portfolio on our own. However, if you are the type who prefers the guidance and occasional hand-holding of a financial advisor when it comes to investing, then do the right thing for yourself and hire a financial advisor to assist you. *But never lose sight of what you are hiring her to do.*

You should be hiring your financial advisor to help you achieve the three fundamental principles of investing —asset allocation, approximating the return of the stock market average and reaching your savings goal. You should *not* be hiring a financial advisor in order to try to beat the stock market average, unless of course that is your specific objective.

The yearly management fees you pay your financial advisor

can be worth every penny if your financial advisor protects you from pushing all the wrong buttons and doing all the wrong things when the stock market moves 1,000 points in either direction tomorrow. A financial advisor's fee is earned by making sure you adhere to your asset allocation goals, not by using your money to attempt to beat the stock market average.

(If you *do* choose to instruct a financial advisor to try to beat the stock market average with your money by investing it in individual stocks and managed mutual funds *just make sure you are keeping score of his actions and selections so you know whether or not you are getting your money's worth.*)

Fees and expenses are not the only thing eating into your portfolio's value. Taxes also have a significant impact on the value of your portfolio at retirement, and the strategy here is really quite simple: If you have an opportunity to reduce your taxes, do it.

How profound.

The most obvious way to reduce your tax bill is to invest in a tax-deferred account, such as an IRA or 401(k) plan, and have your investments grow tax-deferred.

The second way to reduce your tax bill is to own indexed mutual funds instead of managed mutual funds when investing in regular (taxable) accounts. How does this reduce your tax bill? Let me explain.

As a mutual fund owner, you are taxed on any profits made when you sell your shares. You are *also* taxed on the net profits your mutual fund manager generates from all his buying and selling activities — regardless of whether you receive these gains in cash or reinvest them in additional shares.

It goes without saying that if your mutual fund manager is caught up in BUYING LOTS OF THIS and SELLING LOTS OF THAT throughout the year, all his BUY THIS and SELL THAT activity will generate a capital gains tax liability much higher than the capital gains tax generated from an unmanaged index fund. That's because an index fund simply lets the shares in the fund *sit there and do nothing much but grow and compound.*

Let's take a closer look.

A mutual fund's "turnover ratio" is a statistic that gives you a general idea of all the buying and selling activity that goes on within the fund. A mutual fund that has a 50 percent turnover ratio (over the course of a year) can generally be expected to replace (turn over) 50 percent of the portfolio's value.

A mutual fund that has a 100 percent turnover ratio can be expected to replace 100 percent of its value over the course of a year. The table below lists the turnover ratios of the five kinds of managed fund groups and compares them to the turnover ratio of index funds. [5]

| FUND CATEGORY | TURNOVER RATIO |
|---|---|
| SMALL COMPANY | 93% |
| AGGRESSIVE GROWTH | 148% |
| GROWTH | 94% |
| EQUITY INCOME | 68% |
| GROWTH & INCOME | 64% |
| AVERAGE OF ALL MANAGED FUNDS | 87% |
| INDEX FUNDS | 20% |

Even though there isn't a direct correlation between the turnover ratio and capital gains tax liability, the turnover ratio gives you a general idea of the buy/sell activity within a mutual fund — activity that is certain to impact your total return after Uncle Sam gets his chunk of the action.

5. Compiled using Morningstar's software program Principia™ for Mutual Funds. Used with permission.

The table below details the turnover ratio and capital gains tax impact over a five-year period ending December 31, 1997, for the thirteen largest large cap managed mutual funds, compared to the capital gains tax impact for Vanguard's Index 500 mutual fund.

| | TURNOVER RATIO[6] | TOTAL-RETURN FIVE-YEAR ANNUALIZED | PERCENT OF PRETAX PROFIT KEPT* |
|---|---|---|---|
| THIRTEEN LARGEST LARGE CAP FUNDS | 54% | 19.17 | 85.43% |
| VANGUARD 500 INDEX FUND | 5% | 20.12 | 94.20% |

Obviously, when it comes to investing in a regular (taxable) account, it pays to consider owning unmanaged stock index funds, which generally have much lower turnover ratios — and therefore tend to generate smaller capital gains taxes — than managed mutual funds.

Life,
logic,
learning,
investing
and paradoxes.

6. Compiled using Morningstar's software program Principia™ for Mutual Funds. Used with permission.

Oh, and don't forget hoopla.

**hoop•la** (hoop´lä) *n.* *Slang.* 1. Boisterous commotion or excitement. 2. Talk intended to mislead or confuse.[7]

With all the hoopla surrounding what the economy did yesterday, what the stock market did today and which funds to own tomorrow as a result of what happened yesterday and today, don't forget about the expenses and taxes in your portfolio.

If you take the time to figure out how much it costs you, not in warm and fuzzy percentages, but in real dollars, I think you will find that minimizing your expenses and taxes is worth the effort it takes to do it.

7. *The American Heritage Dictionary* (Boston, Ma: Houghton Mifflin Co., 1976.)

WRITING A CHAPTER ON SAVING IS NOT MY IDEA OF a good time.

It would be much more fun to talk about the intricacies of pitching a tent at 14,500 feet on a windy day on the side of the tallest mountain in North America, Mt. McKinley in Alaska (or Denali, for you geography buffs). It is kind of like trying to read the newspaper on the hood of your car while traveling down the freeway at sixty miles per hour in a snowstorm.

Pitching a tent in a snowstorm with the wind blowing at sixty miles per hour is a lot like life: Sometimes you have to make a conscious decision to have fun, because if you don't, it quickly becomes the most miserable experience of your life. In fact, I have taken this concept of consciously deciding to have fun and applied it to other areas of my life, like running out of gas on the freeway, attending the office Christmas party or running the last three miles of a marathon, and I have to say it works pretty good.

The second decision when pitching a tent during a sixty-mile-per-hour snowstorm is a decision to postpone pitching the tent unless the wind calms down or a snow wall is built up. All it takes is one lost tent to decide that this is a smart decision.

After a snow wall is built and the tent is pitched and the temperature hits thirty-five below zero, it's a great feeling to climb inside a sleeping bag that is warrantied to keep you warm for another five degrees.

If there is one thing that is more exciting than building a snow wall and pitching a tent and crawling into a warrantied forty-below sleeping bag in thirty-five-below weather, it's doing all these things and then realizing . . . you have to go.

When it is thirty-five below and you have to go, you go

outside . . .

and go, and then quickly go back inside.

The problem is, you can't go by the tents because if everybody went by the tents there wouldn't be any clean white snow left to melt on the stove the next morning for coffee. When you are hundreds of miles away from the nearest coffeehouse and it is blowing cold and thirty-five below, you best not mess with anyone's coffee. So, every year, a designated go place is established about 100 yards from the tents of the 14,500-foot base camp, causing records to be set all night long in the Denali Invitational 100-yard dash.

Or so it seems.

The real fun though, on Denali, is not building snow walls or pitching tents or forty-below warm sleeping bags or 100-yard dashes. The real fun is getting to 14,500 feet. Fun, that is, if you enjoy carrying a sixty-pound pack and dragging a fifty-pound sled uphill, in the snow and cold, for seven days and twelve miles.

As I recall, the first day was not much fun. Not because of the heavy load. Not because the brutal cold combined with unbearable heat (when the clouds disappeared) made life miserable. The first day was not much fun because of the silence and aloneness.

Silence and aloneness as stark as the white Alaska wilderness.

Silence and aloneness.

During the next few days of nothing but cold, silence and the empty feeling of aloneness, I finally realized I was losing my balance. Not the tip-toe-gingerly-around-a-bottomless-crevasse type of balance, but the back-home-in-Seattle type of balance between family, career and especially myself amidst the clutter of everyday life.

Discussions, disagreements, deadlines, traffic, television, telephones — and you know the rest.

After living this routine for many years, I realized on a cold, desolate mountain, somewhere in the middle of nowhere, I was addicted to the clutter of everyday life, and it finally dawned on me that the clutter in my life might be keeping me from pursuing my dreams and living a life I would choose to live if given a chance to do it all over again. This left me with two options:

Remove some clutter and strike a balance, or pray that someday I would get a second chance.

It's easy to strike a balance on Denali — the balance of sitting tight in a blinding snowstorm and moving higher when the weather breaks, in search of a goal called the summit. The real challenge we face is to strike a balance in the valleys of our everyday lives, because it's in the valleys — not on some desolate mountain — that we pursue our dreams, live our lives and make things happen.

When you get right down to it, removing a little clutter in the process of striking a balance is exactly what saving and spending is all about.

All this important investment stuff like asset allocation, indexing, diversification, tax deferral, compounding, keeping score, rebalancing and living life doesn't do a whole lot of good if we can't strike a balance between saving and spending.

I think you know what I mean.

Now, it might seem like I am oversimplifying the obvious by focusing on saving (and spending) as an important component to building wealth, ignoring Wall Street and getting on with our lives, but as we begin to think about this subject I think you will agree with me that the emotional complexity of saving, combined with the magnitude of its importance, is something many of us need to look at and evaluate.

It seems to me that when it comes to building and maintaining our investment portfolios amidst the chaos that swirls around us, it's easy to bypass the inward responsibility of saving and focus instead on investment things that are out of our control, like daily stock market quotes, quarterly earnings reports and year-end mutual fund summaries, because looking at issues outside of us is a lot easier than dealing with issues inside of us, like our saving and spending habits.

In short, it's much more fun to do a midyear portfolio review than it is to do a midyear personal review.

Striking a balance between spending and saving starts with making a conscious decision to take a step back from the countless activities that consume your every waking moment long enough to calculate approximately how much you should save each month to reach a financial goal. This is something most investors don't do. According to a recent *Wall Street Journal*/NBC News poll, 57 percent of investors have not spent any time calculating how much money they should be saving to reach a retirement goal.

That's quite a few people who are driving in the dark without headlights, hoping to arrive safe and sound at a destination called retirement.

In talking about how much you should save, I am not going to suggest that you radically change your lifestyle, because I know you won't. After all, the lifestyle you are living today is probably the result of a myriad of decisions made over time, including

new jobs,
new homes,
new cars,
new relationships,
new children,
new neighborhoods,
new recreational pursuits
and new dreams.

What's more important than a sudden, radical lifestyle change is being fully aware of the gap between how much you are currently saving and how much you *should* be saving to reach your goal, so that when financial decisions come up in the future, such as buying a new this or a new that, the issue of being responsible for your financial future is at least present at your financial decision-making table.

Then, if the decision to buy a new this or a new that is made today, it is made in an environment in which you are fully responsible for your actions and are able to give yourself full credit for who you are and the decisions you make. The pleasure and satisfaction we derive from being fully responsible for our decisions, and the quiet confidence that comes from knowing those decisions are the right ones, is infinitely more gratifying than the uncertainty of not knowing the implications of our decisions.

The first rule in doing a personal review in order to strike a balance between saving and spending is to do the review in the context of the world we live in, not the world Wall Street lives in. Because Wall Street — and Madison Avenue — are very fond of portraying this retirement thing as gray-haired grandpas and grandmas bicycling through the backroads of France and walking hand in hand on exclusive resort island beaches.

Uh, excuse me.

Having millions and millions of dollars at retirement would be nice, but let's face it, not everyone is going to vacation in the south of France and fly first class the rest of their lives. Some retirees might prefer to do something else.

Keep in mind that the millions and millions of dollars Wall Street says you need at retirement is an arbitrary number created by an industry that has a habit of paying out yearly bonuses of millions and millions of dollars to individual employees. Somewhere along the line Wall Street has forgotten that we can retire and be happy on a little less than millions and millions of dollars.

The problem with using multimillion-dollar retirement figures to compute our savings target today is that this amount can overwhelm us to the point that we are either frozen by inaction or begin to save so rigorously that we miss out on the pleasures of today.

That's why it's important to strike a balance.

Listen: It is not worth making your life miserable today so you can retire in style tomorrow.

Let's face it, most of us are not going to change our lifestyle to the point where we are able to save what Wall Street says we need to save to be happy and enjoy life. I mean, who wants to forego a family vacation next summer, and all the wonderful memories that go with it, so he can save what Wall Street says he should save in order to be rich thirty years from now?

Who knows, you could save all your life for that backroad bicycle trip through France, only to find out those French farmers went on strike again and are letting their cows doodle on the road.

Enough talking about figuring out how much we should save. Let's do it. The ten minutes you spend completing the following worksheet will give you a *general idea* of how much you need to save to successfully arrive at a financial goal sometime in the future, assuming, of course, that you allocate these savings effectively and at least approximate the return of the stock market average with the assets you allocate to common stocks.

It is impossible to know down to the last penny how your investment decisions today will affect the size of your portfolio when you are ready to retire. But completing this worksheet will give you a general idea whether your savings today are in the same universe as your retirement expectations of

# RETIREMENT WORKSHEET

| | ASSUME RETIREMENT AGE AT 65 | 35-YEAR-OLD WITH SALARY OF $52,000 | YOUR NUMBERS |
|---|---|---|---|
| 1 | Annual income needed at retirement in today's dollars (Multiply current salary by 60%) | $31,200 | |
| 2 | Social Security benefits (call 800-722-1313 for estimate, or use 20% of current salary) | $10,400 | |
| 3 | Retirement income needed (line 1 minus line 2) | $20,800 | |
| 4 | Amount of money needed by retirement in today's dollars (line 3 times 18) | $374,400 | |
| 5 | Amount already saved for retirement | $35,000 | |
| 6 | Value of savings at retirement in today's dollars (line 5 times investment growth factor; see following chart) | $157,500 | |
| 7 | Savings still needed in today's dollars (line 4 minus line 6) | $216,900 | |
| 8 | Monthly amount you need to save (line 7 times monthly savings factor listed below) | $260 | |

*Assumes 8 percent growth portfolio, 3 percent inflation and investment in tax-deferred account.*

tomorrow. When you have no idea how your saving habits of today will affect your retirement tomorrow, it is easy to ignore it, because in the short run it is easier to be in the dark about tomorrow than face the facts and do something about it today.

### RETIREMENT WORKSHEET FACTORS

| YOUR AGE | INVESTMENT GROWTH FACTOR | MONTHLY SAVINGS FACTOR |
|---|---|---|
| 19 | 9.9 | .0005 |
| 21 | 9.0 | .0005 |
| 23 | 8.1 | .0006 |
| 25 | 7.4 | .0007 |
| 27 | 6.7 | .0007 |
| 29 | 6.0 | .0008 |
| 31 | 5.5 | .0009 |
| 33 | 4.9 | .0011 |
| 35 | 4.5 | .0012 |
| 37 | 4.0 | .0014 |
| 39 | 3.7 | .0016 |
| 41 | 3.3 | .0018 |
| 43 | 3.0 | .0021 |
| 45 | 2.7 | .0024 |
| 47 | 2.5 | .0029 |
| 49 | 2.2 | .0034 |
| 51 | 2.0 | .0041 |
| 53 | 1.8 | .0051 |
| 55 | 1.6 | .0064 |
| 57 | 1.5 | .0085 |
| 59 | 1.3 | .0119 |
| 61 | 1.2 | .0188 |
| 63 | 1.1 | .0395 |

The best way to subtly remind yourself of the need to save is to make a copy of the above worksheet and tape it somewhere, like your closet door, so that you see it day after day after day. If you have something reminding you day after day after day to do something about a potential financial crisis, eventually you will do something.

Fortunately for many people, this pending retirement problem is ten, twenty or thirty years away. But even though this problem may be ten, twenty or thirty years away, taking personal responsibility for our destiny means having the discipline to do something about it today, even if what you do today is nothing more than completing your worksheet and taping it to your closet door, because the longer you wait to tape it to the closet door the more you delay putting that worksheet into action.

The first step in being a responsible investor is to calculate an approximate savings goal. The next step is to implement your goal, if only a little at first. Following is a graph that points out the importance of saving earlier rather than later. It compares two individuals who save $300 monthly until they reach sixty-five years of age. One starts saving at age twenty-five and the other starts saving at age thirty-five.

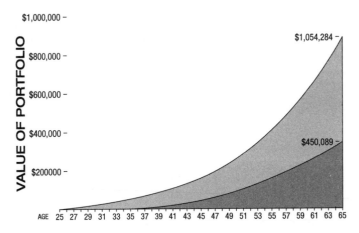

*Example based on 8 percent growth in tax-deferred account*

The investor who starts saving and investing $300 monthly at age twenty-five instead of age thirty-five invests only $36,000 more, but ends up with an additional $604,195 in her portfolio! If you are the thirty-five-year-old and want to start saving, remember that there is one thing much worse than starting to save at thirty-five instead of at twenty-five — and that is to not start at all. You can either sit there and wish you had done something ten years ago, or you can start doing something today and ten years from now look back and be glad you did!

This predicament of inaction is a funny thing, and I suspect many of us have been challenged by it in other areas of our lives in addition to saving and investing:

the inaction of wanting to apply for a new job but not updating the resume,

the inaction of wanting to learn a new skill but not signing up for a class,

the inaction of wanting to say I'm sorry to a friend you've hurt but not picking up the phone.

I have dealt with all of the above at one time or another in my life and I suspect you have also, and isn't it funny that the longer you wait, the harder it is. BUT, when inaction finally turns to action we feel good about the action, whether or not the outcome is in line with our initial expectations, and we find ourselves saying,

"I'm glad I tried."

"I learned a lot."

"It wasn't as hard as I thought it would be."

"At least I know where I stand."

I'm convinced that those of you who take action in the form of saving enough will one day look back with the enormous feeling of accomplishment that usually results from doing something successfully that we know needs to be done.

The following table shows that when you increase your savings amount a little each month it makes a significant impact on the future value of your portfolio. It is a lot easier to save and invest a little more each month than to try to do it all at once at the end of the year.

| MONTHLY INVESTMENT | 10 YEARS | 20 YEARS | 30 YEARS |
|---|---|---|---|
| $100 | $19,497 | $67,290 | $184,447 |
| $300 | $58,490 | $201,869 | $553,342 |
| $500 | $97,483 | $336,448 | $922,237 |
| $1,000 | $194,966 | $672,896 | $1,844,474 |

*Assumes 9 percent growth in tax-deferred account*

While we're talking about the importance of saving, the most efficient way to do it is in a tax-deferred retirement account, such as a company-sponsored retirement plan or your own IRA. When you start your savings program in a tax-deferred account, you are taking advantage of the enormous tax break Uncle Sam offers you by letting your savings grow tax-deferred. And when you invest in a company-sponsored 401(k) plan, many companies will match a portion of your contribution, thus accentuating this tax-deferred growth.

I don't pretend to have all the right answers when it comes to saving enough for one's retirement, because the way we save and increase our savings is different for everyone. For some, sharing a dinner out with their spouse at the end of the month might be a reward for meeting their monthly budget. For others, having dinner out with their spouse might be the punishment for not meeting a monthly budget.

You never know.

The point of this chapter is not to give you a boatload of great savings ideas that you can incorporate into your daily life, like refinancing your home or reusing plastic sandwich bags four times before they are discarded.

Quite frankly, I use them only once.

But I never buy brand-new golf balls.

The point of this chapter is to create an awareness of how our saving today will impact us in the future. I am confident that when this awareness is firmly in place, our sense of personal responsibility, combined with our individual creativity and bright ideas, will find a way to get the job done.

## *8* LET'S HAVE SOME FUN

THERE IS NO WAY I WOULD EVER DRAG MYSELF OUT of bed at 5:45 on Saturday mornings for a twenty-minute walk in the dark and the cold rain to meet up with five friends at a corner coffeehouse table if I didn't think it was going to be a ton of fun.

But it is.

Every time.

With all that life throws our way, we need to take advantage of the fun times — making sure our fun times accentuate our daily experiences as well as our lifetime goals.

And for most of us who are serious about building wealth, ignoring Wall Street and getting on with our lives, I suspect the importance of making the right investment decisions today precedes any great desire to have fun in the stock market. But for some (including me), somewhere deep inside our psyche is a part that wants to whoop it up — you know, get a little more involved in this stock market thing than simply indexing our stock investments and getting on with our lives.

I learned all about having fun in the stock market during my stockbroker days many years ago, from a client I stumbled upon while cold-calling from the yellow pages.

The conversations that evolve from talking to complete strangers who would rather not talk to you are rather interesting, and when you ask that person on the other end of the line to take a chance on your next hot stock idea, it takes a lot of quick talking to get past hello. But one time, a deep, heavily accented voice caught me by surprise and took me up on my offer. After he bought my hot stock idea we watched it go up and up.

It was pretty neat to see my hot stock idea go up and up, because with each proceeding phone call I had a sense this person was thinking I was a pretty hot stock picker. The more I think he thinks I'm a pretty hot stock picker the more I believe it, and before long I think therefore I am.

The exciting part about being a pretty hot stock picker is that the new client gives you a chance to pick another hot stock and gosh, this stock doesn't just go up, it also goes down. One day this client decided to change the subject from stock market things and invited me to climb a mountain.

I thought to myself, I don't want to climb a mountain, maybe I could get this guy to caddie for me instead.

But my client was persistent, and one month later, on a Saturday morning, I was halfway up a glacier on the side of a mountain in northern California.

Cold, hungry and thirsty.

After making it to the top of that miserable thing, I vowed never to climb another mountain in my life. Unfortunately, things don't always go as planned, because back at my desk in Seattle a big white thing called Mt. Rainier kept smiling at me.

Yeah, yeah, yeah.

A couple of months later, while coughing, shaking and shivering on top of Rainier, I vowed again to never climb another mountain. A few mountains later I stopped making those vows, because vows just get you in trouble anyway.

Climbing a mountain has little to do with hanging by a thread hooked to a ledge near the side of a cliff. Climbing a mountain has a lot to do with putting one foot in front of the other, slowly and methodically, even when you don't feel like it, until there's only one way to go — down, because you have reached the top.

After noticing I had mastered the art of putting one foot in front of the other much better than I had mastered the art of picking stocks, my persistent client called and said, "Let's climb Mt. McKinley!"

What?

Climb the tallest mountain in North America? Climb one of the coldest mountains in the world? Climb the mountain they call Denali that killed twenty people the previous three years? Forget it. Think golf balls.

Six months later I discovered that the major difference

between climbing Denali and climbing Rainier was the thickness of one's underwear and the thinness of one's patience with that person you're stuck with in a tent for three weeks.

You will notice that the more I talk about my mountain-climbing prowess the less I talk about my stock-picking prowess, because while I was climbing up the mountains my client's stocks were going down the tubes.

One day I asked this client of mine why he continued to invest in my stock ideas with the same devil-may-care attitude with which he climbed mountains. He replied, matter-of-factly, "It's fun!"

Hmm, okay. So maybe you just wanna have fun.

If you want to have fun in the stock market there is one simple rule to follow: Make sure you — not some mutual fund manager — is the one having fun. When you turn your money over to a mutual fund manager in pursuit of a little fun and excitement in the stock market, you are defeating your purpose. The mutual fund manager ends up being the one having fun — at your expense — and you give up any realistic chance of beating the stock market over the long term. How boring — and how dumb.

But what the heck, let's see what happens when we *do* turn our money over to a mutual fund manager in pursuit of a little fun. Let's invest $500 a month for twenty years in the average actively managed mutual fund (which, incidentally, has underperformed the stock market average by 16 percent annually over the five-year period ending 1997[1]) and compare it to an investment in an unmanaged index fund that mirrors the Wilshire 5000 Index:

At the end of five years, your actively managed mutual fund is trailing the index fund by $3,320.
*Are you having fun yet?*

At the end of ten years, your actively managed mutual fund is trailing the index fund by $18,175.
*Are you having fun yet?*

At the end of fifteen years, your actively managed mutual fund is trailing the index fund by $56,916.
*Are you having fun yet?*

At the end of twenty years you are now ready to retire and

1. Compiled using Morningstar's software program Principia™ for Mutual Funds. Used with permission.

your actively managed fund is trailing the indexed portfolio by $142,549.

*Are you ha . . .*

Oh, forget it.

The point is, if you are making a million dollars a year and at the end of the year are getting paid million-dollar bonuses, like the presidents and CEOs of most financial institutions, I guess you are entitled to have a little fun in the stock market.

But when you are getting up each morning and struggling to get your children to school on time so you can make it to work on time and trying to figure out how you can make it to two different soccer games that night — and you are doing all you can to save and invest $500 a month in your 401(k) and trying to find another $500 a month to put in a college education fund for your little soccer stars, and you know that if managed mutual funds continue to underperform the stock market average as they have in the past it could cost you hundreds of thousands of dollars at retirement —

uh, maybe we should take our fun elsewhere.

If you want to have some fun in the stock market, the

solution is not to turn your money over to some mutual fund manager. The solution is to first index the majority of your stock market assets to make sure most of your money is at least keeping up with the stock market average and then take a *small* portion of your stock market money and invest it in your own common stock ideas . . .

and have the time of your life!

There are many reasons why you might want to take a little detour on this journey and invest in individual common stocks. Some of us (including me) love to gamble, and I suspect that the rush of adrenaline one gets when placing a chip on red is not unlike buying a hot stock that makes widgets and gizmos and then watching it go from two to twenty and back down to two again (after we've sold it at nineteen and five-eighths, of course).

Yet the more I ponder the possibility of a correlation between investing and gambling, the more I am inclined to think there is a stronger force than gambling luring so many investors to pick individual stocks. This force is a fundamental desire to compete. After all, the strength of our country is built on the freedom to compete and win, compete and lose, pick yourself up and compete again. I love to compete as much as anyone, whether it's in business or basketball, and I have found that the best way to pass the time during a five-day snowstorm is to play a little poker in the tent.

But the main reason I enjoy picking my own individual stocks with a small portion of my total portfolio is because I want to be part of a particular company that has a successful product or service that has evolved over time from an explosion of bright ideas.

All we have to do is look around us to see this explosion of ideas unfolding before our eyes. I am reminded of this explosion of ideas every time I sit down to do some work on my personal computer, because next to my personal computer, which has a word processor attached to a spreadsheet program attached to a database management program hooked up to a laser-jet printer, is my 1923 Underwood typewriter. I doubt if there has ever been a time, a place or a country such as ours that has provided such a dynamic opportunity for creative human beings to take a 1923 Underwood typewriter idea and sketch it and mold it and alter it and transform it into something called a technology revolution.

Ideas that arise from our essential creativity — they just keep coming, one after the other, and the ideas of yesterday that are obsolete today barely have time to get out of the way for the better ideas that are germinating today and will be ready to go tomorrow.

One of the best examples of people putting their essential creativity to work through an explosion of new ideas is in the American automobile industry — an industry that once upon a time many people had given up for dead.

This was a big industry with big problems, but its workers realized that *creativity was essential for survival.* To see an industry that was so down in the dumps and losing out to competition from another corner of the world stand up and not only survive but succeed — big time — is what essential creativity is all about. And for those investors who stood up with them and invested in this industry's essential creativity, it paid off — big time.

Even though this investment journey has shown us that the best way to build a successful common stock portfolio is to forego investing in individual companies in favor of investing in our country's collective creativity, this journey wouldn't be complete if we didn't address that part of our emotion that enjoys the challenge of investing in the great ideas and great products of individual companies.

This doesn't mean we need to become "stock market junkies" who are completely caught up in the workings of the stock market and subscribe to newsletters, read mutual fund magazines, attend financial seminars, watch financial television shows, trade on the Internet and calculate account values daily. This part of the journey is for investors who realize the importance of approximating the stock market average with the majority of their stock market investments but still want try their hand at buying a few stocks here and there because after all, it can be fun and challenging to pit your wits against everyone else in the stock market. And who knows? Somewhere among the millions and millions of stock pickers might be the next Warren Buffett.

But I'm not sure it's worth risking your entire portfolio to find out you aren't.

The important thing to remember, when pitting your wits against everyone else, is to keep your emotions of fear and greed in check so that your stock market fun remains fun, because when fear and greed aren't controlled, buying and selling individual stocks can quickly become a miserable experience.

Let's look at a few ways you can fulfill the need to have fun in the stock market without allowing it to adversely impact your overall stock market portfolio.

- Pick stocks, not mutual funds, and pick them yourself. If you pick mutual funds, you allow a mutual fund manager to pick stocks for you, which defeats the purpose of having fun in the first place.

- Start by investing no more than 5 to 15 percent of your total portfolio in stocks. A larger commitment than this could significantly impact your total investment return.

- At year-end, compare the return of your stocks with the return of the stock market average. This comparison will either give you an appreciation for the difficulty of outperforming the stock market averages, or it will give you a chance to brag about your stock-picking prowess.

When looking for stocks to buy it helps to remember that a stock is much more than a three-letter symbol in *The Wall Street Journal.* It is a share of a company, with a headquarters made up of people who get up in the mornings and put in a hard day's work to make that company successful.

With that in mind, it's a good idea to invest in companies

you know and understand. For instance, if you have first-hand knowledge that a company's employees not only enjoy working at the company but provide a service or product that is in continual demand, chances are you are going to be much more successful investing in the common stock of that company than you would owning a no-name company halfway across the country that you are unfamiliar with.

For example, if I were to buy into a company with my fun money, I might choose Nordstrom, because I appreciate their commitment to customer service, and I know for a fact that customer service keeps Nordstrom's clients coming back. I might buy Microsoft because I have edited this book what seems like 6,000 times on Microsoft software, and for some reason I like a company whose product helps me transform my dreams and ideas into realities. I might buy Boeing, because I like the way their employees listen to their customers and build airplanes to fit the needs of the airline industry.

For me, the important thing in owning Nordstrom, Microsoft and Boeing is not to get caught up in all the stuff Wall Street gets caught up in, because if I get caught up in Wall Street stuff like fifty-two-week highs and lows, price-earnings ratios and long-term debt, I am likely to underperform the stock market average the way mutual fund managers do. The problem with putting these three companies under a microscope and analyzing all the fifty-two-week-long-term-price-earnings-book-to-ratio stuff like Wall Street does is that you tend to lose sight of the fact that these companies have great products, great customer service and, most importantly, great people.

I mean, who really cares if Nordstrom is expanding too fast, Boeing is having temporary production problems and Microsoft is knocking heads with the fed. If companies that have great products, great customer service and great people continue to grow their products and accentuate their customer service by embracing the great ideas of their employees and customers, more often than not they will be around another twenty-five years and their success will eventually be reflected in my portfolio.

For the most part it makes sense to invest in companies you can easily understand. It doesn't take a rocket scientist to understand the necessity of Boeing airplanes (no offense to all the great rocket scientists at Boeing), Nordstrom's attention to detail or the usefulness of Microsoft software.

On the flip side, in my neighborhood is headquartered a

biotech company with a crazy name like Bioenzymintrixnex, Inc., or something. I don't follow this company, in fact, I haven't a clue what they do, and with a name like that I'm not sure I want to find out, but I do know it has never turned a profit and I don't know if it ever will.

When it comes to picking a stock for the fun portion of my portfolio, this company is not for me. But that is not to say this isn't a great investment, because maybe you are the type of investor who is willing to take time to visit the headquarters and talk with the employees to learn more about their company, and maybe after learning about it you decide that even though they are not making any money today, this company has a great product or idea and is worth the risk.

In this situation, the chance of you losing some or all of your money is much greater than the chance of me losing some or all of my money in Nordstrom, Microsoft or Boeing.

That's the downside.

However, this biotech company might enter into a joint venture next month with an international conglomerate that takes its product or idea and markets it all over the world, and your initial investment ends up going up 1,000 percent next week. That's the upside.

Isn't all this upside/downside stuff fun?

Once you buy a company you like, that's when the real fun begins. Anybody can buy a stock. It's the decision of whether and when to sell it that gets a little hairy. Don't you just love those stories heard down at the neighborhood coffeehouse about Uncle Joe's great aunt's nephew's first cousin's neighbor's wife, who bought shares of Proctor & Gamble ninety-three years ago and still owns the same shares that over the years have grown and multiplied like jackrabbits and are now worth more than a million jackrabbits? If you never hold onto a stock long enough to let that "through-the-roof" stock go through the next roof and the roof after that, you give up the opportunity to be the topic of discussion at some future neighborhood coffeehouse because your desire to book a profit caused you to sell too early.

The sell decision on a "through-the-roof" stock is complicated because you will kick yourself if you sell and it continues to go through three more roofs, but you will kick yourself harder if you don't sell and it proceeds to drop through the floor.

The decision on whether and when to sell a stock that drops through the floor is a little more emotional, because it implies we made a mistake in deciding to buy the stock in the first place, and sometimes it is hard for us to admit we made a mistake. But heck, having the courage to admit we made a mistake is half the fun of picking your own stocks, because it makes those through-the-roof discoveries so much sweeter. Once you do sell, it frees you up to take that money and look for another through-the-roof stock.

When evaluating whether or not to sell a stock, it helps to make the decision in the context of what the stock market did during the time period you owned the stock. If your common stock is down 20 percent during a five-month period but the stock market average is down 15 percent during the same five-month period, a decision to sell the stock and cut your losses may be a bit premature, because your stock hasn't been a complete disaster compared to the stock market average.

If you begin to notice that all your buy decisions should have been sells and all your sell decisions should have been buys and you start to get frustrated, remember — the goal is to have fun.

Most of our lives are a little chaotic. The challenge of building wealth, ignoring Wall Street and getting on with our lives can appear intimidating and insurmountable. It doesn't have to be. When we unclutter one part of our life, we enrich another part, and that is what this investment journey is all about. When we simplify investing, we take another step toward discovering our contagious spirit and our unique energy in such a way that we impact our world, making this a better place for everyone. I suspect that's what most of us would say life's all about.

I wish you the best of luck.

## STOCKS

The following table is a partial list of index funds, divided into categories. Call the individual companies for details.

| CATEGORY | INDEX TRACKED | MINIMUM PURCHASE | MIN. IRA PURCHASE | PHONE |
|---|---|---|---|---|
| **TOTAL STOCK MARKET INDEX FUNDS** | | | | |
| VANGUARD INDEX TOTAL STOCK MARKET | WILSHIRE 5000 | $3,000 | $1,000 | 800-662-7447 |
| FIDELITY SPARTAN TOTAL STOCK MARKET | WILSHIRE 5000 | 15,000 | 15,000 | 800-544-8888 |
| T. ROWE PRICE TOTAL EQUITY MARKET | WILSHIRE 5000 | 2,500 | 1,000 | 800-638-5660 |
| **LARGE COMPANY STOCK INDEX FUNDS** | | | | |
| DOMINI SOCIAL EQUITY | DOMINI 400 | 1,000 | 250 | 800-762-6814 |
| DREYFUS S&P 500 INDEX | S&P 500 | 2,500 | 750 | 800-373-9387 |

| CATEGORY | INDEX TRACKED | MINIMUM PURCHASE | MIN. IRA PURCHASE | PHONE |
|---|---|---|---|---|
| FIDELITY SPARTAN MARKET INDEX | S&P 500 | $10,000 | $500 | 800-544-8888 |
| GALAXY II LARGE CO. | S&P 500 | 2,500 | 500 | 800-628-0414 |
| SCHWAB S&P 500 | S&P 500 | 1,000 | 500 | 800-435-4000 |
| SSGA S&P 500 INDEX | S&P 500 | 1,000 | 250 | 800-647-7327 |
| T. ROWE PRICE EQUITY INDEX | S&P 500 | 2,500 | 1,000 | 800-638-5660 |
| USSA S&P 500 INDEX | S&P 500 | 3,000 | 2,000 | 800-382-8722 |
| VANGUARD INDEX 500 | S&P 500 | 3,000 | 1,000 | 800-662-7447 |
| **SMALL COMPANY STOCK INDEX FUNDS** | | | | |
| DREYFUS S&P 600 | S&P 600 | 2,500 | 750 | 800-373-9387 |
| FIDELITY SPARTAN EXTENDED MARKET | WILSHIRE 4500 | 15,000 | 15,000 | 800-544-8888 |
| GALAXY II SMALL CO. | S&P 600 | 2,500 | 500 | 800-628-0414 |
| SCHWAB SM.CAP | SCHWAB SM.CAP | 1,000 | 500 | 800-435-4000 |
| VANGUARD SM. CAP | RUSSELL 2000 | 3,000 | 1,000 | 800-662-7447 |
| **INTERNATIONAL INDEX FUNDS** | | | | |
| DREYFUS INT'L STOCK INDEX | MSCI EAFE | 2,500 | 750 | 800-373-9387 |
| FIDELITY SPARTAN INT'L INDEX | MSCI EAFE | 15,000 | 15,000 | 800-544-8888 |
| SCHWAB INTERNATIONAL INDEX | SCHWAB INT'L INDEX | 1,000 | 500 | 800-435-4000 |
| VANGUARD TOTAL INTERNATIONAL | MSCI EAFE | 3,000 | 1,000 | 800-662-7447 |

| CATEGORY | INDEX TRACKED | MINIMUM PURCHASE | MIN. IRA PURCHASE | PHONE |
|---|---|---|---|---|
| **LARGE COMPANY VALUE FUND** | | | | |
| VANGUARD INDEX VALUE FUND | S&P/BARRA VALUE | $3,000 | $1,000 | 800-662-7447 |
| **LARGE COMPANY GROWTH FUND** | | | | |
| VANGUARD INDEX GROWTH FUND | S&P/BARRA GROWTH | 3,000 | 1,000 | 800-662-7447 |
| **SMALL COMPANY VALUE FUND** | | | | |
| VANGUARD SMALL CAP VALUE FUND | S&P SM. CAP 600 BARRA VALUE INDEX | 3,000 | 1,000 | 800-662-7447 |
| **SMALL COMPANY GROWTH FUND** | | | | |
| VANGUARD SMALL CAP GROWTH FUND | S&P SM. CAP 600 BARRA GROWTH INDEX | 3,000 | 1,000 | 800-662-7447 |

As an alternative to mutual funds, investors can own the S&P 500 Index in "common stock" form by purchasing Standard & Poor's Depository Receipts, or SPDRs (Spiders). For more information, call the American Stock Exchange at 800-THE-AMEX.

## BONDS

You can invest in either bonds or bond funds. Although they have similar features, these are strikingly different investments. Bonds have a stated maturity when the face value of the bond is redeemed and returned to the investor. Bond funds, on the other hand, don't have a stated maturity. Consequently, if interest rates rise due to a stronger economy, your bond fund will decline in value, and it might be twenty years (if ever) before interest rates decline enough for the value of your bond fund to return to 100 percent of your original investment.

For some reason, I can't get excited about something that might *never* return to its original investment due to an increase in the productivity of our country. Nevertheless, bond funds have become an enormously popular and convenient investment tool for owning bonds.

The best bond funds to own are indexed bond funds, because the fees are so low. We discovered in chapter 6 that expenses on stock mutual funds can significantly impact the total return over time. When it comes to investing in bond funds, fees are even more important because they generally eat up a greater percentage of your annual income. The following is a list of indexed bond funds.

| CATEGORY | TYPE | MINIMUM PURCHASE | MIN. IRA PURCHASE | PHONE |
|----------|------|------------------|-------------------|-------|
| **BOND FUNDS** | | | | |
| GALAXY II U.S. TREAS IDX RET | INTERMEDIATE GOVERNMENT | $2,000 | $1,000 | 800-628-0414 |
| DREYFUS BOND MKT. INDEX INV. SHARES | LONG-TERM BOND | 2,500 | 750 | 800-373-9387 |
| VANGUARD BOND IDX SHORT-TERM | SHORT-TERM BOND | 1,000 | 1,000 | 800-662-7447 |
| VANGUARD BOND IDX INTERMEDIATE-TERM | INTERMEDIATE TERM BOND | 1,000 | 1,000 | 800-662-7447 |
| VANGUARD BOND IDX LONG-TERM | LONG-TERM BOND | 1,000 | 1,000 | 800-662-7447 |

For investors who want to invest in U.S. Treasury Securities, check the following Website for a step-by-step guide to buying them, current auction information and downloadable forms: http://www.publicdebt.treas.gov. Or call: 800-943-6864.

# ADDITIONAL READINGS

Bogle, John. *Bogle on Mutual Funds: New Perspectives for the Intelligent Investor*. Burr Ridge, IL: Irwin Professional Publishing, 1993.

Hazan, Marcella. *Essentials of Classic Italian Cooking*. New York, NY: Alfred A. Knopf, Inc., 1992.

Hogan, Ben, and Herbert W. Wind. *Ben Hogan's Five Lessons: The Modern Fundamentals of Golf*. Trumbull, CT: Golf Digest, 1985.

Lindbergh, Anne M. *Gift From the Sea*. New York, NY: Panthenon Books, 1991.

Malkiel, Burton. *A Random Walk Down Wall Street: Including a Lifecycle Guide to Personal Investing.* New York, NY: W.W. Norton & Company, Inc., 1995.

Siegel, Jeremy J. *Stocks for the Long Run.* Burr Ridge, IL: Irwin Professional Publishing, 1994.

Waterman, Jonathan. *Surviving Denali: A Study of Accidents on Mount McKinley, 1903-1990.* Boulder, CO: American Alpine Club, 1991.